FROM LO]

Nick Brown

Prologue

"So, why an American road trip?" I hear you ask.

"Is there not enough for you in any of the states the good old US of A has to offer? Could you not decide where to go? Are the golden beaches of Florida or California not enough for you? Is there not enough excitement in New York or Miami? Aren't the New England states charming enough? What on Earth are you playing at, man…?"

Woah, there! So many questions…

The seeds were sown a couple of years back. To cut a long story short – (actually, it's not really a long story, just a bit complicated although, come to think of it, it isn't really that complicated, either) – I had to go over to Italy to rescue my mum and dad.

Ooo, that sounds a bit drastic, doesn't it, "rescue my mum and dad"? I mean, it's not like they had been kidnapped in a fiendish plot and smuggled overseas or anything like that. I didn't even have to slip in at the dead of night under the cover of darkness in a covert operation like I was working for the British Secret Service. Actually, I did slip in at the dead of night under the cover of darkness but that was more by necessity than design, due to a delay with the ferry.

Anyway, I digress. Me and my mate Alex answered an SOS from my mum to go over to Italy to bring them back home as my dad had been taken ill on the cruise they were, up until then, enjoying. They had been left in a hospital in the port of Civitavecchia near to Rome with no way of getting back to England. Our plan was to get the ferry to Calais, drive through France, down into Italy, rescue the parents and return. As it turned out, we were a little longer in Italy than anticipated before my dad recovered enough to be able to go home again and it was thought best that they would fly home rather than endure the long drive.

As you can imagine, the return trip back to Blighty was a lot more enjoyable and comfortable than the outward leg as we no longer had the worry of not knowing in what sort of state we would find my parents. As we made our way back up through Italy and France, we found that it was actually quite good fun. It was here that the idea of a road trip – a proper road trip – came about.

We quickly decided on the Pacific Highway along the coast of California. This was in part due to the song 'Let The Monkey Drive' by the music duo Sparks. It's a particular favourite of ours, with the opening line being 'We're drive north on Highway 1 towards Santa Barbara, lots of sun, Pacific Ocean on the left hand side'. And that, really, was that. An idea was born.

When we got back and told our wives of the plan, their responses ranged from the sarcastic "You can afford that, can you?" to the bolshie "Go on then, we're not going to stop you" via the hilarious "What, you two? You'll get lost and end up in Alaska in the middle of nowhere! Ha ha ha…"

(To be fair, when they realised it was something we had really thought about, they were very supportive.)

After a little planning and shopping around for the best deals, the idea of ditching the Pacific Highway in favour of the historic Route 66 seemed ever more appealing. Funnily enough, we hadn't thought of it originally but, when suggested as an alternative, we just seemed to fancy the idea more and more. And who wouldn't want to drive almost 2,500 miles across the United States, Chicago to Santa Monica? I mean no offense to the Pacific Highway, but the 66 is three and a half times the length. I'm sure there are some really nice places and beautiful scenery along Highway 1, Malibu is an obvious attraction and I'd love to see San Francisco, but just the thought of cutting right through the heart of the country east to west through big cities, small towns and, for the most part, the unknown, at least for us, is just too much of a temptation to turn down.

Route 66 was established in November 1926 and has become one of the most famous roads in the world. It was recognised in popular culture by the song '(Get Your Kicks) On Route 66', originally composed by the jazz pianist Bobby Troup and made famous by Nat King Cole, whilst other recordings were made by Bing Crosby, Chuck Berry, The Rolling Stones and Depeche Mode amongst others.

John Steinbeck's Pulitzer Prize winning novel 'The Grapes Of Wrath' sees the Joad family leave their home in Oklahoma to escape drought and poverty to travel to Los Angeles during the Great Depression of the 1930s. It was in the pages of 'The Grapes Of Wrath' that Steinbeck called Route 66 'The Mother Road', a nickname that has stuck to this day.

The television show 'Route 66' ran on US television between 1960 and 1964, and the highway also provided inspiration for the Disney film 'Cars'.

And there we have it. Flights and car booked, hotel rooms reserved, excitement level at fever pitch. With everything in place, we head off to Heathrow Airport bound for Chicago. Route 66 here we come. Let's see if it lives up to all the hype and we do indeed get our kicks…

(And yes, my dad was fine, thank-you very much for asking)

Chicago, Illinois

"I've just blown in from the Windy City, the Windy City is mighty pretty, but it ain't got we we've got, no sireee...."

But it does have quite a bit, to be fair. Traditionally, Chicago has an awful lot of ingenuity and innovation. For example...

- The world's first ferris wheel was constructed for the Chicago World Fair in 1893
- The first vacuum cleaner – nicknamed 'The Whirlwind' – was invented in Chicago
- The first reliable, not the very first, but the first *reliable*, dishwasher is Chicagoan
- And thank-you, Mr Ike Sewell, for the deep pan pizza!

We touched down at Chicago O'Hare International Airport at lunchtime, early one sunny May afternoon. Due to the time difference, our flight from London Heathrow had only taken two and a half hours, even though it had actually taken eight and a half hours.

Time differences always fascinate me. Concorde used to take an average of three and a half hours to get from London to New York. *Three and a half hours!* This means that passengers would have arrived two and a half hours before they had taken off. Actual time travel. But what about this to blow your mind... in 1996, the fastest ever trans-Atlantic flight was recorded when Concorde arrived in New York a mere two hours and fifty three minutes after leaving London. So, with the time difference taken into consideration, if you had stayed on that plane and it had immediately returned to London at the same speed, you would actually have arrived back 14 minutes before you took off on your outward flight. This means that when you touched down you would see the plane you were in across the runway waiting to take off and you might even see yourself boarding the plane!

But what would happen next? Would you be caught in a time-loop and live out the rest of eternity continuously flying across the pond, climbing down the steps of one plane and then climbing up the steps of another (the same) plane? Or would you carry on with your day as normal, meaning that there would, from then on, be two of you – one in London and one in New York? And what would happen if, at some point in the future, you actually met each other? Would it have caused a massive time paradox and started the universe folding in on itself?

I'm talking rubbish, of course, it would never happen, it's an impossibility. Or is it…?

Anyway, returning to the matter at hand, we touched down at Chicago O'Hare International Airport at lunchtime, early one sunny May afternoon. After collecting our baggage and successfully getting through customs, we headed out to the car rental company. I had booked an 'intermediate' vehicle for our journey. According to the advertising, an 'intermediate' vehicle is suitable for couples or families, providing comfortable rides no matter how long the journey. That's ideal, then. Although we're not a couple in the traditional sense, there were two of us so, technically, that is a 'couple'. We were given a catalogue from which to choose our vehicle and flicked through the pages of decent family cars suitable for a nice run-around. There was nothing wrong with any of them, they were all cars perfectly capable of doing what we needed them to do, but we both knew what the other was thinking…

"Mate, we're about to do Route 66, it's the trip of a lifetime, I don't really want to do it in a Peugeot 108."

I have to say at this point that there is absolutely nothing wrong with a Peugeot 108, it is a perfectly good car to get you about town but getting about town we ain't. A quick scan of some of the cars available – and it was a quick scan because we only turned a couple of pages before pointing and saying "that's the one" – led us to a jet black Dodge Challenger. Now, I'm not really a car person. As long as it looks ok, works and gets me to where I want to go, that would generally that ticks my boxes. However, when we were taken outside to give the Dodge the once over, my immediate reaction was "oh yes, I could be seen in this!" Alex, on the other hand, *is* a car person and as soon as he saw it his grin was so wide it almost knocked his ears off. It was like someone had offered him the Batmobile for two weeks. Love at first sight.

*

We spend the weekend in Chicago before heading off on our voyage of discovery, so there was a bit of time to explore. Our first impression was that Chicago was a really nice place. Considering it is a big city, it didn't really have that big city feel, like you'd get in somewhere like New York or London. It was a lot more 'homely'.

Speaking of being homely, upon our meanderings we came across the Elephant And Castle pub. What? Why is this here? The Elephant And Castle is an area in south London, famous for its unusually brightly coloured shopping centre, its statue of an elephant with a castle on its back at the transport hub, and for being the birthplace of both Charlie Chaplin and Michael Cain. Obviously, we had to go in. The irony wasn't lost on us. We'd flown 4,000 miles from London and had our first meal in a pub named after a place 60 miles from our doorstep.

The Elephant And Castle was exactly what we imagined an American 'English style' pub to be – a central square shaped bar not unlike the one featured in 'Cheers', with televisions on the walls all tuned in to different sports. The baseball was on and we got talking to a couple (this time a 'couple' in the traditional sense) decked out in their Chicago Cubs uniform, complete with caps. They had apparently tried and failed to get tickets for the game against the New York Yankees at the famous Wrigley Field so were here watching it on TV instead. They tried to convince us that baseball was the greatest game on Earth whilst we were expounding the virtues of a game of football. When I say 'football' I obviously mean English football, rather than American football (how can you call it football when you use your hands...?)

I also owe the Elephant And Castle a big thank-you. Some people like a glass of whiskey, some prefer gin but my particular tipple is vodka, and it wasn't too long before we noticed that one part of the bar had about 20 different flavoured vodka liqueurs lined up. Strawberry flavour, lime flavour, melon flavour, etc, but then we noticed a whipped cream flavour. Whipped cream flavoured vodka? Whoever thought of that in the company's planning meeting? Various fruit flavours go without saying, caramel and butterscotch, no problem, but whipped cream? It goes without saying that we had to try one, and it was just lovely, exactly like liquified whipped cream with that little vodka kick of heat (job done, and done jolly well). Upon returning home I tried to find a bottle in the English supermarkets but, alas, had no joy. That was until my younger daughter's wedding when she and the groom presented me with a bottle as a little present. I tell you – that stuff is yummy!

My wishing to try the said tipple also led to one of my favourite conversations I have ever had...

Me: "Can I try a whipped cream flavoured vodka, please?"

Bartender: "Certainly, sir. What would you like with it?"

Me:	"Er, I'll have a bag of potato chips. What flavours do you have?"
Bartender:	"No, I mean with the vodka."
Me:	"Eh?"
Bartender:	"What mixer would you like?"
Me:	"Mixer?"
Bartender:	"Yes. Soda? Ginger Beer?"
Me:	"But surely if I have a mixer with it, it'll ruin the whipped cream taste, won't it?"
Bartender:	"You mean you want it neat?"
Me:	"Well, yes. I want to see what it actually tastes like."
Bartender:	"Wow – you're brave…!"

A trip to Chicago isn't complete without a visit to Navy Pier. Stretching out onto Lake Michigan, Navy Pier is one of the most popular tourist attractions not only in Chicago but in the whole mid-west. There's no admission fee to the pier itself but some of the attractions and shows may charge their own entry prices. Along the pier you'll find a whole host of eateries, museums, theatres as well as areas to just sit and drink in the view which, incidentally, is fantastic. Whilst we were there the weather was lovely, as it was for the whole trip. With the sun gleaming off the lake and the Chicago skyscrapers in the distance stretching up into a cloudless sky, it really was a stunning sight.

*

It's worth mentioning the size of Lake Michigan. The lake's area is roughly 22,400 square miles and is the largest lake in the world that is in a single country. Two of the other 'great lakes', Lake Superior and Lake Huron, are bigger but they are in both America and Canada. It is bigger than nine of the fifty states. Just think about that. A lake is bigger than nine of the states.

Next morning, after breakfast, the time had arrived. We could travel from Chicago to Los Angeles using the interstate highways, but what is the point in that? We wanted to drive on Route 66 for every inch possible. As the highways were being built, more and more of the route was being decommissioned, but most of the road still remains. In 1985 the end finally came and the route as a whole received its decertification and US-66 officially ceased to exist. Bits of the 66 were actually overtaken by the new faster roads so for these parts we have no choice but to use them. Fortunately, though, these are few and far between, with the vast majority being as was. When not detouring off into towns of varying size, much of the longer stretches run parallel to the highways whilst other sections seem to be in the middle of nowhere.

US Route 66 was one of the original highways when the US Highway System was inaugurated (but more about that a little later). It was established in 1926, running through eight states – Illinois, Missouri, Kansas (albeit it for only 13 miles), Oklahoma, Texas, New Mexico, Arizona and California. After the advent of the big interstate highways, though, the road was removed from the US Highway System but the mystique lives on.

Route 66 is all about the history and – and I hate myself for daring to utter such a cliché – its all about the journey rather than the destination. Every day, every few hours, you are at a completely different place to the one you've just left. Big cities, little towns, interesting and important places historically, crazy places that make you wonder what goes through some people's mind, ghost towns … they're all here along the route. Throw some quirky roadside attractions into the mix and what's not to love? Or at least to experience?

So then, here we go. The 'Route 66 Begin' sign, and therefore the start of our journey, is on the corner of South Michigan Avenue and East Adams Street, just across the way from Grant Park on the shores of Lake Michigan. Full of excitement for the adventure that lay ahead, we took the statutory photo by the marker, jumped into our hired Dodge Challenger (did I mention that?) and embarked on the 200 or so mile stretch to Springfield, our first overnight stop.

The two intrepid explorers set off. The valiant and heroic pioneers from a foreign land commenced their voyage of discovery into territory hitherto unexplored, at least by them, not knowing what would await them on their epic expedition. We pulled away along East Adams Street, traversed the intersections with South Wabash Avenue and South State Street and turned left into South Clark Street. It was at this point, after driving for very nearly half a mile, that we realized we'd taken the wrong turn.

Well, this bodes well, doesn't it!? So back to the start we go. At this rate we'll barely have left Illinois before our return flight leaves, let alone traverse almost two and a half thousand miles across the third biggest country on Earth…!

Springfield, Illinois

The drive from Chicago to Springfield provided one of those stretches where the interstate highway borrowed the old Route 66 road. We had to use the I-55 for a while coming out of the Windy City although, helpfully, sporadically along the road there were signs telling us we were on Historic Route 66.

We were taken through a town called Wilmington. The town's most famous resident is a giant spaceman. Known as the Gemini Giant – named after the Gemini space programme – he is 30 feet tall, wears a green space suit and holds a rocket in his hands. He stands outside the Launching Pad Restaurant. The Gemini Giant is one of a series of Muffler Men situated throughout the States. Muffler Men are giant ⬚iberglass statues that are used for advertising or just as curiosities. The first of such figures was crafted in 1962 as promotion for a café in Flagstaff, Arizona, and many more followed. The term Muffler Men is a nickname given them in the 1990s by the founders of the website www.roadsideamerica.com who, whilst cataloguing roadside oddities, noticed that many of the giants were outside vehicle repair shops and holding mufflers, or exhaust pipes as we Brits call them. The name stuck. When businesses who had a Muffler Man either closed or moved on, the statues were often repainted to represent their new tenants.

*

We came off the highway not long after Wilmington at a town called Gardner and it was here that we first experienced the old 66. Just outside the town is a junction that, if you took the turning to take you back towards Chicago, there is a crumbling piece of road that takes you through fields towards the Mazon River, the only turn-offs being into driveways up to farm houses. Just before the river, the road suddenly ends and driving any further would have you crashing into the trees of the wildlife area.

Turning round and driving back towards the junction, the road is suddenly a lot more maintained and also suddenly deserted. All the other traffic is still on the highway and it becomes obvious why Route 66 was decommissioned. Any business worth it's salt is of course going to utilise the faster three or four laned roads as it transports it's freight from one place to another, it's reputation would depend on it. I mean, if you were a customer, which company would you use? The one that continued to use the old single lane road or the one that got your order to you twice as quick? But for us, though, for the first time on our journey, we are alone on the Mother Road and the adventure had begun.

The route took us through Dwight, Odell, Pontiac, Chenoa and Lexington before arriving at a town called Normal. This, of course, was hilarious to us and it elicited the expected response from our wives when we sent back a picture of the 'Welcome To Normal' sign.

"They didn't let you in, then? Ha ha ha."

Yeah, yeah, yeah, nice one, we didn't expect that...!

Normal is a metropolitan municipality with Bloomington. In the 1820s the first non-native settlers arrived – the Kickapoo Indians were the original residents after migrating from the Great Lakes region – and changed the name from Keg Grove to Blooming Grove (there is a Keg Grove Brewery in Bloomington). Many farming families were attracted to the area due to the fertile soil and the town's economy grew on agriculture, with Abraham Lincoln amongst those who would come to the area to trade while he was still working as a lawyer.

In the 1850s North Bloomington began to take shape and the Illinois State Normal University was established there in 1857, specialising in training future teachers. The term 'Normal School' comes from the French 'Ecole Normale', a school set up in Reims, France, by Jean-Baptiste de la Salle to train scholars to be able to provide education to the poor. Today, Normal Schools are more often known as Teacher Training Colleges. With the heavy French influence in Illinois – they were the first European settlers in the area to make contact with the natives – the word 'Normal' was naturally inserted in the name of the university and North Bloomington just became known as Normal as a geographical reference for those attending the university.

Exiting Bloomington, the route ran alongside the I-55, separated only by a grass verge. This was the case for most of the rest of the way to Springfield, our first overnight stop along the way.

Springfield, the state capital, is an important place politically. In 1837, a 28-year-old lawyer called Abraham Lincoln moved to Springfield and a few years later was elected to the US House of Representatives. His famous Peoria Speech, in which he outlined legal, moral and economic arguments against slavery was possibly, above all else, the thing that propelled him on the road to the Presidency. If you were to tour the city you would be able to visit the Abraham Lincoln Presidential Museum, that Abraham Lincoln Presidential Library, his former home and also his tomb which is in Oak Ridge Cemetery.

Nearly 147 years later, Senator Barak Obama stood on the steps of the Old State Capitol in Springfield to announce his candidacy for the White House.

The city's original name was Calhoun after Senator John Calhoun, and the first dwelling was a cabin occupied by one John Kelly in 1818 after he discovered that wild game and deer freely roamed the area. Today there is a marker on Jefferson Street where his cabin stood. By 1821 Calhoun was made the county seat and when settlers from Virginia, Kentucky and North Carolina arrived the city began to develop. The change in name to Springfield occurred due to John Calhoun, who had been serving as Vice President of the United States under both John Quincy Adams and Andrew Jackson, falling from favour and resigning his position.

*

Springfield also saw a fair bit of action during the Civil War. As Commanding General, Ulysses S Grant trained his regiment there and new businesses and railways were constructed to help support the war. Also, the first official death in the Civil War was that of a Springfield resident, Mr Elmer Ellsworth. When the war ended, Springfield became a major hub in Illinois' railway system and Ulysses S Grant went on to be elected President in 1865.

Aside from all the political machinations, Springfield is home to the Cozy Dog Drive-In. Situated on South Sixth Street, part of the route's original alignment, the Cozy Dog has been a Route 66 fixture since 1950. For those who are uninitiated, a cozy dog is, basically, a hot dog on a stick. The story goes that when studying in Oklahoma, a young man called Ed Waldmire came across a somewhat unusual sandwich of a hot dog sausage baked in cornbread. So intrigued was he by this, that he spoke of it to one of his fellow students whose father was a baker, but that was that. Or so he thought. Five years later, when serving in the Air Force, Waldmire received a letter from his student friend telling him that his father had developed a mix that would stick on a sausage and wondered if Waldmire would try some. Using cocktail forks for sticks, Waldmire called his invention Crusty Curs. His friend continued to send him batches of the mix and he sold hundreds of them. Upon returning to Springfield, he rebranded them and a legend was born. Actually, it's a little inaccurate to say he rebranded them, as it was actually his wife Virginia who insisted on the rebranding, maintaining that Crusty Cur was a silly name and she came up with Cozy Dog instead. Not only that, but she also designed the famous Cozy Dog logo of two hot dogs hugging each other. They opened a stand selling the Cozy Dogs outside their home which proved to be extremely popular and, due to the demand, Ed and Virginia looked for business premises from which to trade. The Cozy Dog Drive-In has been on old Route 66 ever since.

The first thing we did when arriving in Springfield was to find and book in to our hotel. We had reserved a room at the Hampton Inn and, when we arrived, we found that directly opposite was a substantially large shopping unit. "That might be useful," we thought, "we can pick up some snacks for the journey, perhaps some potato chips, chocolate bars and the like." However, on closer inspection, we discovered it was signposted as 'Firearms Super Centre'.

Ah. Obviously we knew that guns are available to American citizens but, a Firearms Super Centre right next to our hotel which was, incidentally, tucked away round a corner from the main street, wasn't top of our list of local attractions we wanted to see. As it turned out, nobody attempted to shoot us. Well, I say nobody attempted to shoot us, they might well have but, fortunately, nobody who was a decent aim tried to shoot us.

We awoke the next morning (thank goodness), had our breakfast and set off for St Louis. A short drive along the I-55 and then off to a frontage road that was part of the old route. This stretch was not exactly what you would call excellently maintained but that mattered not to us. We were hoping there would be twists and turns and bumps and jolts and, although this wasn't quite that bad, it was strangely pleasing.

We traversed the town of Litchfield, past the Ariston Café, one of the oldest (it itself claims to be *the* oldest) on the entire route and, when out the other side, the road was a little bit more car friendly. It was also far enough from the highway for it to be really quiet and we were all alone. Only every so often would another car go past. This is what we wanted!

We crossed the border from Illinois into Missouri over the Mississippi River via one of the many bridges available to use. Unfortunately, the Chain Of Rocks Bridge wasn't one of them. The bridge used to be the method Route 66 traffic crossed the river but, alas, no more. Originally built as a toll bridge, the Chain Of Rocks Bridge, named for the rocky rapids called the Chain Of Rocks that make that particular bit of the Mississippi hazardous for river going vessels to navigate, was designated part of the 66 in the 1930s. It took commuters around St Louis to avoid the downtown area, whereas the MacArthur Bridge, now used for railroads, was used as the city route in. As traffic increased, however, the road was forced to reroute for the sake of both safety and convenience and the Chain Of Rocks Bridge closed in 1968. It would have been demolished but for a local group called

Trailnet who leased the bridge, renovated it and it is now open again but only to pedestrians and cyclists.

Our entry into Missouri was made across the McKinley Bridge and from there it was just a short journey to our hotel.

St Louis, Missouri

There's a lot to see in St Louis. Some other big cities that I could mention are pretty faceless and you could pick them up and drop them anywhere else and they would just be exactly the same as they were before. St Louis, though, is not in this category. It most definitely has it's own personality and ambience.

One of the most famous, certainly one of the most instantly recognizable, monuments in America is the Gateway Arch. It is the world's tallest arch, the tallest man-made monument in the western hemisphere and Missouri's tallest accessible building. Known as the Gateway To The West, it was originally built as a monument to the western expansion of the United States. There is an underground visitors' centre and the observation area at the top of the arch offers stunning views over the city and the Mississippi River.

(I couldn't help thinking that if they build another one right next to it and painted them yellow, then a certain fast food franchise would have the greatest advert in the world...)

St Louis also has a claim in inventing rock 'n' roll. Whilst not necessarily absolutely inventing it from scratch, the St Louis scene of the 1950s certainly helped bring the genre into the mainstream.

Chuck Berry was born in St Louis in 1926 and became one of the most influential musicians in the history of popular music. His first single 'Maybelline' sounded like nothing else and his sound, developed from rhythm and blues but given a more rebellious feel with guitar solos and lyrics that often centred around teenage life, paved the way for rock 'n' roll as we know it. Hits such as 'Roll Over Beethoven', 'No Particular Place To Go' and 'Johnny B Goode' cemented his legend. He was the first person to be inducted into the Rock And Roll Hall Of Fame.

The Delmar Loop, a cultured district just outside of the city, has a bronze statue of Chuck Berry as one of its centrepieces along what is described by the American Planning Association as "one of the 10 great streets of America". As we walked along we noticed that they have their own version of the Hollywood Walk Of Fame for famous St Lousianans. Aside from Chuck Berry, there are stars for people such as the writer TS Eliot, tennis star Jimmy Connors, singer Tina Turner and many others, old and new. The Loop is so called not because it actually is a loop but because the streetcars loop around the area before continuing on their journeys.

The history of the Delmar Loop would be an awful lot different if it wasn't for a local businessman called Joe Edwards. He and his wife Linda opened the Blueberry Hill restaurant in 1972 with the goal of running a place that would be welcoming to everybody, with good food and a cold beer or two in an atmosphere of music and memorabilia. And it wasn't long after opening that they realised they needed to help revitalise the whole area, not just their own restaurant.

In the beginning, Mr and Mrs Edwards had a hot dog machine, a decent beer selection and a collection of – so they say – 30,000 records that they alternated on their jukebox. I have to say, to me this sounds absolutely ideal. However, move on they did and, as the restaurant became well known, their menu expanded and Blueberry Hill became famous for its burgers. The Elvis Room was opened in 1985, hosting live music evenings and was joined in 1997 by The Duck Room, named after Chuck Berry's signature move. The Duck Room came about during a conversation between Edwards and Berry during which Chuck reminisced about the smaller, intimate clubs he used to play in when he was just starting out on the road the superstardom. Chuck Berry himself played over 200 gigs in the Duck Room and other musical luminaries such as John Legend, Ed Sheeran and Grandmaster Flash have also appeared. It continues to be used as a live venue.

Joe Edwards was behind the St Louis Walk Of Fame and he has also had a hand in renovating and opening other Delmar Loop icons such as the 1920s-era Tivoli Movie Theatre, Pin-Up Bowl – a bowling alley and cocktail lounge -, the Moonrise Hotel with its famous roof-top bar and the Peacock Diner.

*

As we strolled up and down Delmar Boulevard, we couldn't help noticing how friendly the people there were. Tables were on the pavements (sidewalks?) outside eateries and bars, and the people there just seemed to be having a good time. There were lots of smiles and laughter and "hi there"s and, when our accents were noticed, more than once we became involved in little chats about why we came to St Louis, what we were doing whilst we were there, and there was a good amount of whooping and excitable shouts of "yeah" thrown our way when we said we were doing Route 66.

Had we more time than our itinerary had allotted us, the Delmar Loop is certainly one of the places where we would have spent more time. As it was, we had just the one afternoon to explore St Louis and, of course, there was more to see than just the Loop, much as we liked it and enjoyed the ambience. If I ever return to St Louis, the Delmar Loop would certainly be one of my hang-outs with all the other kool kats.

Our hotel was only a short distance from Busch Stadium, home of the St Louis Cardinals baseball team so we had a wander round. Ballpark Village, right next to the stadium, has sports bars (naturally), a Budweiser brew house (Budweiser is the main product of Anheuser-Busch who have a big contract with the Cardinals, hence the name Busch Stadium) and a Cardinals Hall Of Fame. I imagine the atmosphere is good when there's a game on, especially if the Cardinals are on a winning run. I always thought that one of the most exciting things about going to a football match in England (yes, *proper* football, remember what I said in Chicago…?) was the hour or so before kick-off. We used to come out of the London Underground station nearest to the stadium and as soon as we hit street level, especially if it was a nice sunny day, the atmosphere was just brilliant. The crowds would be chanting, the programme and merchandise sellers would be shouting out their own special slogans, the smell of the burger stands would come wafting down the road, the feeling of confidence about the afternoon's match in the air…fantastic!

Speaking of Anheuser-Busch, before setting off the following morning for our next stop, there was enough time to visit their HQ. The brewery offers the public free tours ending with a sample of your chosen tipple in the Hospitality Room. And a jolly interesting tour it was, too.

The origins of the brewery go back to 1860 when William D'Oench and Eberhard Anheuser purchased the Bavarian Brewery, which was on the brink of bankruptcy. The following year, Anheuser's daughter married a local wholesaler named Adolphus Busch and he began working as a salesman for his new father-in-law. A few years later D'Oench sold his share of the company to Busch whose business acumen soon came to the fore. He was the first American to use pasteurization to keep the beer fresh and also the first to use mechanical refrigeration and refrigerated railroad cars. Business boomed. In the 1870s Busch toured Europe to study changing brewing methods and, upon his return, they started the manufacture of Budweiser. So successful was it, and so successful were they in transporting it across the country, that Budweiser became the United States' first national beer brand. In 1879 the company was renamed Anheuser-Busch and, upon Anheuser's death the following, year Mr Busch became the President (ooo, that sounds familiar, doesn't it?). The Busch family remained in control through the generations until 2008 when the company was sold to InBev in a $57 billion deal that merged the two companies, creating the world's largest brewer. In addition to Budweiser and Michelob that were being produced by Anheuser-Busch, the newly formed Anheuser-Busch InBev also had Stella Artois, Labatt and Becks on its portfolio amongst others. Truly a mega company.

Something else I didn't know about Anheuser-Busch was the existence of the famous Budweiser Clydesdale horses. The tour took us to their paddock. The Clydesdale tradition began in 1933 when August Busch presented his father with a team of Clydesdales to celebrate the repeal of the Prohibition. It proved to be an excellent publicity stunt as the horses took the first two barrels of post-Prohibition beer to the Mayor of St Louis. Later that year they were in Washington DC to deliver a further two barrels to President Franklin Roosevelt. Today the horses make many appearances pulling the Budweiser beer wagons behind them.

Since the late 1970s it has also become tradition that the Budweiser Clydesdales appear at the opening home game of the St Louis Cardinals' season. Each year the horses emerge from the players' tunnel and make a lap of the stadium accompanied by organ music playing 'Here Comes The King', an advertising jingle written for Budweiser, 'the king of beers'.

The route from St Louis to Springfield again, as is understandable when exiting a large city, meant us travelling, at least at first, along a section of the highway, this time the I-44. As we drove, we couldn't help noticing that every so often there was a billboard at the side of the road featuring Jesse James, the outlaw of times past. 'Come And Visit Jesse James Territory', 'The Jesse James Trading Post', 'The Jesse James Wax Museum', 'The Jesse James Ice Cream Parlour', 'The Smell Of Gun-Smoke – A New Album Of Country Classics From Jesse James'.
(Only some of those were real…)

Jesse Woodson James was born in Clay County, Missouri, in 1847. Due to the heavy migration of southerners from Kentucky and Tennessee, Clay County and it's neighbours became known as Little Dixie. The southerners naturally brought with them their social, cultural and agricultural practices and so, that being the case, when the American civil war erupted in 1861, the James family held southern sympathies. Jesse's older brother Frank joined a pro-Confederate group of guerrillas known as the Bushwhackers, operating in Missouri and Kansas and, when

Frank's squad arrived back in Clay County, 16-year-old Jesse also signed up.

The leader of that particular group, Fletch Taylor, lost his arm to a shotgun blast and the James brothers joined a group led by William Anderson, known as Bloody Bill. The group was involved in some particularly nasty incidents, including the Centralia Massacre in which they attacked a train carrying Union soldiers, scalping and dismembering some of the victims. After Anderson was killed in a separate ambush, the James brothers went their separate ways. Jesse was severely injured after being shot in the chest by a Union patrol in Lexington, Missouri, and was taken to his uncle's boarding house in Harlem to recover. There he was tended to by his cousin Zerelda Mimms, and they began a courtship that ended in their marriage nine years later.

Jesse James, as we know, went on to become one of the legendary figures in American history. His name is ranked alongside those of the likes of Wild Bill Hickok, Buch Cassidy and Billy The Kid in the outlaw annals of fame. It was on 7 December 1869 when he first came to national attention, when he and an accomplice (thought to have been Frank) robbed the Daviess County Savings Association in Gallatin, Missouri. They didn't get away with much money but it was the shooting of the cashier, John Sheets, that caused the headlines. Jesse mistakenly thought that Sheets was Samuel Cox, the man who had killed Bloody Bill Anderson, and shot him in revenge. The Governor of Missouri, Thomas

Crittenden, offered a reward for Jesse's capture and his legend was born. Six months after the robbery, the Kansas City Times printed the first of a series of letters from Jesse James addressed to the public claiming his innocence. He captured the readers' interest and Jesse James' celebrity was born.

The James brothers gained national notoriety, with their gang robbing banks and stagecoaches. They joined forces with Cole Younger and his gang and carried out a series of robberies in one place after another, their territory covering not only Missouri and Kansas, but stretching to Iowa, Texas and West Virginia. They robbed banks and stagecoaches, often even playing up to bystanders.

Their downfall began on 7 September 1876 in an attempted raid on the First National Bank of Northfield, Minnesota. The robbery went badly wrong and only Jesse and Frank escaped with either their lives or their liberty. Cashier Joseph Heywood had refused to open the safe and the townsfolk outside had become suspicious of the men guarding the door to the bank. As the gang fled, a shootout ensued between the gang and the locals. Whilst the militia accosted the bandits, the James brothers escaped back to Missouri. Jesse formed a new gang, robbing stores and trains but, once again, the numbers were soon reduced and they were down to Jesse and Frank and another set of brothers, Charley and Robert Ford.

The Ford brothers moved in with Jesse at his request but, unbeknown to Jesse, the brothers had contacted Governor Crittenden and concluded a deal to collect a full pardon for their criminal activity in exchange for their killing their host who was, by now, the most wanted man in America. On 3 April 1882, whilst standing on a chair to dust a picture hanging above the mantlepiece, Jesse James was shot in the back of the head by Robert Ford. His death caused a national sensation, so much so that crowds of people came to his house to see him lay there dead. Governor Crittenden kept his word and the Ford brothers, after being sentenced to death by hanging, were granted a full pardon.

The most persistent of all the Jesse James billboards were the ads for Meramec Caverns, apparently the hide-out of Jesse James. As we got closer and closer to the town of Stanton, the billboards appeared more frequently – 'Meramec Caverns 10 miles', 'Meramec Caverns 9 miles', 'Meramec Caverns 8 miles', etc.

The Caverns, situated on the Meramec River, are a series of limestone caves, first developed during the American Civil War when they were mined for saltpetre, a mineral used in the manufacture of gunpowder. Their commercial value was first recognised by one Mr Lester Dill or, more accurately, Master Lester Dill.

Young Master Dill was only eight years old when his father Thomas ventured into the caverns – in particular Fisher's Cave –

and it obviously had an effect on him because by the age of 10, Lester was taking tourists in on guided tours with just his old kerosene lamp to light the way. The caves continued to be of interest to Dill over the years until he and his wife Mary tried to make their fortune in oil in Oklahoma, real estate in Florida and carpentry in St Louis. They returned to the Meramec Valley in 1928 when Thomas was made Superintendent of the Meramec State Park and the caves became an official tourist attraction.

When the Great Depression of the 1930s hit, Lester Dill started to search for his own cave to develop into his own tourist attraction to, hopefully, earn him a few pennies. He decided to take a lease out on Saltpetre Cave. The reason he settled on this particular one was for two reasons…

Firstly, the history of the cave intrigued him. It was said that Spaniard Hernando De Soto discovered the cave in 1542 and, during the 1800s, the cave was used by miners for storage and shelter and legend has it that local slaves who had escaped their owners would shelter there before making their way to the relative safety of the northern states. And not only did runaway slaves hide there but the stories were that outlaws, including Jesse James, also used it as a hideout.

The second reason for Lester Dill's interest was the cave's proximity to Route 66. His idea was that the travellers and tourists would jump at the chance of a bit of exploration. He renamed his attraction Meramec Caverns and hired local labourers to construct a road leading right to the cave. The

Caverns opened for business in 1933 and he eventually purchased the property, putting his entire energy into making the operation a success. His family even lived there in a tent for a while. His business acumen was so that he made sure visitors to the Caverns would leave with a car bumper sticker advertising his venture. In 1940, Dill discovered some old rusted guns and an old chest in a hitherto unknown part of the cave, which he immediately claimed had been the property of Jesse James. Needless to say, the legend 'Jesse James' Hideout' was now associated with the Caverns.

Perhaps the greatest piece of publicity for the Caverns – and, in fact, pretty much anything else – centred around Jesse James himself. The reports of his death and how it had happened were a bit too mundane and not heroic enough for many of his admirers and over time a series of old men came forward claiming to actually be the outlaw himself. They claimed the corpse of Jesse James wasn't the corpse of Jesse James but, of course, one by one, their stories were proven to be full of holes. There was one particular gentleman, however, whose story captured the attention of Dill's son-in-law, Rudy Turilli.

John Frank Dalton, from Oklahoma, was the latest in the line of Jesse Jameses to come forward. His story was that, instead of shooting James, Robert Ford had actually killed a different member of the gang called Charles Bigelow who was then buried under the pretence of being Jesse James in order to allow James to live out his life in peace. James, ie: John Frank Dalton, was now a bedridden old man and decided it was time to confess to what had really happened. Apparently, Jesse James' gang and Missouri Governor Crittenden had all been in on the ruse and had made a pact to only disclose their true identities when they reached 100 years of age.

The local press in Oklahoma were seemingly starting to believe the story as it appeared that no reporter was able to find any discrepancies in what Dalton was claiming. And, as Meramec Caverns were now using the name of Jesse James in its advertising, Rudy Turilli travelled to Oklahoma to meet Dalton. If Jesse James was in fact still alive, it would be a publicist's dream. When he got there, he was amazed at what he found.

Quite understandably leaning on the sceptical side, Turilli examined Dalton and discovered that his body seemed to have the correct damage to actually be that of Jesse James. The tip of the index finger on his left hand was missing, his right eyelid drooped, there were bullet scars on his left shoulder and there was evidence of severe burning on his feet. Stunned yet thrilled with what he had seen, Turilli brought Dalton back to Stanton with him and gave him a cabin at Meramec Caverns. Whilst there, reporters wouldn't leave him alone and Turilli himself also became a celebrity, appearing on television and in newspapers and magazines desperate to prove the legitimacy of Dalton's claim. He even offered $10,000 to anybody who could prove Dalton was a fraud. So much publicity was created that a Jesse

James Wax Museum was built in Stanton. Dalton died in 1951. If he was who he claimed to be, he was just short of his 104th birthday.

The big question then ... was John Frank Dalton actually Jesse James? As tends to be the case in this sort of thing – (oh come on, listen to me! "This sort of thing" indeed. How often does somebody claim to be a long-dead Wild West legend?) – there are those that say post-mortem examinations prove his claims and there are those that say they disprove his claims. If it was false and all one massive publicity stunt then I really, really admire that. What a stroke of genius by Mr Turilli that would have been. On the other hand, I really hope it was true. I mean, how brilliant would that have been!? It'd be like Elvis reappearing to say a final farewell before being taken by old age or Bigfoot getting fed up with hiding in the Olympic National Forest in Washington and being discovered on a bus heading for Seattle to rent a condo for his retirement.

You know what the saddest thing about this whole story is? It's the fact that we didn't know what Meramec Caverns actually were. Had we realised, it would have been a must-see attraction. I love all that Wild West, cowboys, outlaws stuff. In fact, Cowboy Land, as I have called it, is the theme of another road trip I have planned. How interesting would it be to visit Deadwood and sit in the same saloon as Calamity Jane and Wild Bill Hickok; to see the site of the Battle of the Little Bighorn and relive of Custer's

Last Stand (without actually being shot); to walk through the streets of Tombstone and explore the OK Corral, the sight of the famous shootout involving the Earp brothers, Ike Clanton and Doc Holliday..!?

(Of course, when I say "another road trip I have planned", this depends on my actually being able to afford it. Sadly, I'm not holding out much hope…)

After passing the Caverns, pretty much the rest of the route to Springfield was on the old Route 66 without touching the interstate, which meant trying to avoid the cracks and potholes. The road took us through a town called Bourbon which was one of the many places en route that sprang up when the railroads were being built. The construction brought settlers to the area who were able to obtain some land at a very reasonable price. A town was proposed and construction workers moved in and set up camps and a general store was opened. The store imported barrels of Bourbon for the construction workers (presumably when they were off duty rather than when they were working otherwise who knows what some of the buildings might have looked like). A barrel labelled 'Bourbon' was left on the porch of the store and the workers would go to 'Bourbon' whenever they fancied a snifter, and soon the area just became known as Bourbon.

I like that little story. I like it when places come about in that sort of way rather than just being named after a particular wealthy benefactor or whatever.

The houses on the part of the old 66 that cuts through Bourbon are generally small, practical single storey places with porches for the residents to sit out on. There is no pretention about them and Bourbon really has that old time feel about it. It's as if we are actually driving the route during Steinbeck's 'Grapes Of Wrath' era.

After leaving Bourbon the route runs alongside the I-44 for a while until it veers through the town of Cuba (oh look – the Jesse James Market Place!). A short while after exiting Cuba we came to a community called Fanning. I call it a community because it's far too small to be called a town. As far as we could tell, Fanning is pretty much just a single street through which cuts the 66 with one or two other lanes branching off that. There is one thing, though, that made us stop...

The 66 Outpost was opened in 2007, providing snacks, hunting supplies and Route 66 souvenirs. It closed for a while in 2016 due to economic reasons, but was soon purchased and re-opened. It wasn't the store that made us stop, though, it was what was outside the store. Created in 2008 and standing 42 feet high and 20 feet wide is what is advertised as the world's largest rocking chair. Yes, that's right, a rocking chair. It can actually swing back and forth as can a standard rocking chair but, for safety reasons, it is chained down. Nowadays it is actually only the world's second largest rocking chair, having been superseded by a 56 footer in Casey, Illinois, in 2015. Whether Casey suffers from 'small town syndrome' or not, I can't say, but it is also home to the world's largest wind chimes, wooden shoes, crochet hook, knitting needles, pitchfork, mail box and golf tee!

Anyway, first or second, the rocking chair at Fanning is one of those things that make you think "why?" whilst at the same time being a great thing to see. I'm a sucker for that sort of thing. If its big, brash, bright and bizarre it will instantly have my attention. (Note to self … visit Casey.)

Continuing on Route 66, the road condition continuously changed from decent to ok to nothing more than a pathway and then back to ok again. The nearer we were to any of the towns, the more upkeep the road looked to have had, but as soon as we were outside limits it reverted back to 'let's just leave it, no-one's going to come through here anymore'. It's this variety that really brought home to us just how neglected the route, or at least sections of the route, has become. I mean, you can understand it because, with next to no traffic using it, why would you pump millions into keeping it in top notch condition? It did make for a really interesting drive, though.

Springfield, Missouri

It is here that the story began.

In 1925, the American Association Of State Highways approved a scheme for marking the interstates, and the creation of a road stretching all the way from Chicago to Los Angeles was put forward by Cyrus Avery, chairman of the Oklahoma Department Of Highways, and John Woodruff, an entrepreneur from Springfield, Missouri. Together they mapped out the route, deliberately including within their plans towns and rural areas that had no major road running through them. Avery insisted that the road be given a round number and proposed that it be designated Highway 60. Delegates from Kentucky, though, also had their eye on the number 60, wanting it for the road between Virginia Beach to Los Angeles, as no roads ending in 0 passed through Kentucky. After much negotiating – or should that be arguing? – Kentucky was given the number 60, with 62 being 'awarded' to the Chicago to Los Angeles route. Shortly afterwards, however, Avery noticed that the catchy sounding Route 66 was unclaimed and he sent a telegram from the Colonial Hotel in Springfield saying they would like the number 66 and his proposal was accepted.

On 30 April 1926, the official designation of Route 66 was given to the Chicago to Los Angeles road in Springfield, Missouri, and the legend was born. The Colonial Hotel is unfortunately no longer with us, though, having been pulled down in 1997.

Upon the official creation of the new highway system, Avery founded the US Highway 66 Association in 1927 with the purpose of getting the 66 completely paved and also to promote the highway with a view to attracting as many visitors and tourists as he could. Woodruff was elected the Association's first President and they went on a publicity offensive, advertising in magazines, brochures and on billboards. They even organised what they called the Bunion Derby, a foot race from Los Angeles to New York (I know, I know). The race began in LA on 4 March 1928 and the winner, Andy Payne, reached the finish line in Madison Square Garden some 573 hours, 4 minutes and 34 seconds of running time later, on 26 May. He was rewarded with a first prize of $25,000. This I find it beautifully ironic that the winner of the Bunion Derby was A Payne…!

The US Highway 66 Association's campaign was an outstanding success and the road was fully paved in 1938.

This wasn't Springfield's first entry into the history books, though. On 21 July 1865, the town square at Springfield entered legend. It was here that the dual between Davis Tutt and Wild Bill Hickok took place.

Hickok and Tutt had previously been friends but their relationship soured after a falling out over a woman. Isn't this always the way? Things came to a head when Tutt coached and supplied money to Hickok's opponents in a card game. Hickok was doing well, winning what was, essentially, Tutt's money. This obviously didn't go down too well and Tutt kept reminding him of previous debts, with the pair inevitably disagreeing on amounts owed. Tutt grabbed Hickok's pocket watch and left. He proceeded to appear in public on several occasions wearing the watch, demanding Hickok pay $45 for it in payment of debts, even though Hickok insisted he owed only $25. They finally faced up to each other in the town square. Both drew, both shot, Tutt missed but Hickok didn't.

Hickok was arrested and put on trial for manslaughter. The jury acquitted him on account of Tutt initiating the fight by taking the watch and witnesses also testified that it was Tutt who drew first. It was this incident that turned the hitherto unknown Wild Bill Hickok into the legendary figure we know today. Ten years later he took a wagon train to a town called Deadwood in South Dakota. One of the other passengers was a lady by the name of Martha Jane Canary, known to her friends as 'Calamity'. They struck up a friendship and a beautiful musical was born.

And even that, ladies and gentlemen, is not all. As if being the birthplace of the world's most famous road and the sight of one of history's most famous shoot-outs wasn't enough, Springfield can also claim to have the world's first drive through restaurant.

In 1947, Sheldon Chaney – known as 'Red' due to the colour of his hair – purchased a gas station and added a café. He soon deduced that passers-by might well enjoy the convenience of buying a burger without leaving their automobiles. So, to cater for such ones, he cut a window in the side of his restaurant and the drive through was born. I wonder how the conversation went that day…

Red: "I'm just doing a bit of DIY, dear…"

Mrs Red: "Really? Well, don't let me stop you! What are you doing?"

Red: "I'm just cutting a hole in the side of the restaurant."

Mrs Red: "Woah there, Red. You're doing what?"

Red: "I'm cutting a hole in the side of the restaurant. It's for people who want a burger but don't want to get out of their cars. They can just drive up, give the order and away they go."

Mrs Red: "Are you off your head?"

Red: "You're not keen, then?"

Mrs Red: "I forbid you to destroy my restaurant!"

Red fires up his chainsaw

Mrs Red: "It'll never catch on…"

Our overnight stay in Springfield was the Route 66 Rail Haven Motel. It has a real '50s feel about it with its nostalgic décor and some themed rooms. It was this motel, incidentally, that once played host to a young up-and-coming rocker called Elvis Presley. He appeared in Springfield on 17 May 1956 to promote his new album, just as he hit the number one spot for the first time with his single 'Heartbreak Hotel'. He and his mum checked into the motel for the duration of his stay in the city. Who was to know that he would go on to become the King of rock and roll? And no, 'Heartbreak Hotel' wasn't about the Rail Haven, but I bet he left them 'All Shook Up'. What do you mean I made this whole story up so I could make a few Elvis puns? You've got 'Suspicious Minds', haven't you? 'Don't Be Cruel'. Oh, come on, give me a break – 'It's Now Or Never' for the Elvis gags…

Actually, now that I'm thinking about it, I realise that I have a lot in common with Elvis Presley. Elvis stayed at the Rail Haven Motel, had a string of hits around the world that are still well known today, sent millions of young female hearts a-flutter, had a singing voice that was smooth as silk, was an icon of style and cool and was a man. I have also stayed at the Rail Haven Motel and am a man. Uncanny, huh?

The next morning, after a hearty breakfast of cereal, pancakes and OJ (oh yeah, I've got the lingo), we bid a fond farewell to the Rail Haven and proceeded on the next leg of our trip towards Oklahoma City. We had only been going a few minutes when we passed one of the curiosities Springfield has to offer. Having seen the world's (second) biggest rocking chair yesterday, today it was the turn of the world's biggest fork. The fork, made of stainless steel, stands 35 feet tall and is stuck into the ground outside the offices of The Food Channel. If you wanted to eat with it, incidentally, going by the measurements of a standard dinner fork, which is about eight inches, and keeping to the same proportions, you would have to be roughly 315 feet tall. You would also have to have a massive plate of food otherwise a fork that size would be no good to you whatsoever. Forget having just a steak, you would have to dine on the entire cow!

Upon leaving Springfield, the route was fairly busy until the 66 turned away from the I-44 and then, once again, we were pretty much lonesome travellers ('Are You Lonesome Tonight'? No, sorry, the Elvis reference are done). We also started going through places with some really interesting names like Albatross, Rescue and Plew, all of which seemed to have a population of about 14. We'd pass two or three residences and then that would be it, out the other side again. We snaked through Carthage and Joplin before crossing the state line into Kansas at Galena.

Galena the town was founded when galena, the mineral form of lead sulfide, was discovered in 1876. The owner of the land where it was discovered, a German farmer by the name of Egidius Moll, began negotiations with local mining companies in nearby Joplin and before long the place burst into life. Incorporated the following year, the influx of miners, businessmen and people just hoping to make a quick buck swelled the population to over 10,000, and at the turn of the century that figure had risen to 30,000. When Route 66 was established along the town's main street it served to add to Galena's prosperity as more travellers passed through and hotels, shops and restaurants opened up. The town's popularity lasted until the early 1970s when the mines finally ran out of lead and zinc and Galena went into a rapid decline. The miners moved away, the sudden loss of a big amount of the population had a detrimental effect on the local businesses and Galena's importance came to an end as quickly as it had originally started.

Before reaching Baxter Springs, we drove over Rainbow Bridge. Constructed in 1923, the bridge has been listed on the National Register Of Historic Places. The bridge is a single-span concrete arch and is the only one of its kind left on the route. Due to its age and the amount of traffic, another bridge has been constructed but, hey, as if we weren't going to go over the original one!

The Café On The Route – that's its name, I'm not expecting you to just know which one I mean out of the hundreds there must be on the 2,500 mile journey – occupies the building that was once the Cromwell Bank. Guess what happened there in 1876? I'll give you a clue … it was robbed. I bet you can't guess who carried out the robbery, though, can you? Oh, hang on, you can – Jesse James. Man, that guy got about, didn't he!?

Over the boarder in Oklahoma, the route took us through miles and miles of farmland, broken only by the occasional small town. We parked up in Vinita as the main street looked to us a bit like a film set. The buildings could have passed for facades but, no, it turns out they were real. One of those buildings – actually, this one does look real – is Clanton's Café. Opened in 1927 by Grant

Clanton, it is the oldest continually owned family restaurant on the whole of Route 66.

Oklahoma City, Oklahoma

The history of Oklahoma as a state, at least in the early days, is one full of political manoeuvrings and machinations. In 1830, President Andrew Jackson passed the Indian Removal Act, allowing him to make treaties with the various tribes east of the Mississippi River for their territories in exchange for new land further west. Dozens of tribes of varying sizes were reassigned. Included in these were what were labelled the Five Civilized Tribes, the Cherokee, Chickasaw, Choctaw, Creek and Seminole. The European Americans labelled them 'civilized' due to their literacy in English and their consenting to intermarriage with the white Americans. The others, who for some unknown reason weren't jumping for joy that their culture and whole way of life was about to be changed forever, were obviously uncivilised because of it. The reassignment didn't go as smoothly as the government hoped, though, as the Seminole treaty was declared illegitimate by the majority of the tribe, resulting in the Seminole Wars after which the survivors were paid to move. Also, only 2,000 Cherokee migrated westward, with 16,000 remaining behind. This resulted in 7,000 soldiers being sent in to force the move, without even giving them time to collect together their belongings. Their march west became known as the Trail Of Tears as 4,000 Cherokee died on the way.

In May 1890, the Oklahoma Organic Act was passed creating Oklahoma Territory alongside Indian Territory. Oklahoma

Territory contained land given to various tribes including Apache, Cheyenne, Kickapoo and others, along with some unassigned land, whilst the vast majority of Indian Territory contained the Five Civilized Tribes, with others crammed into the north-eastern corner. The Act also allowed for homesteaders to be granted land in the unallocated areas via a land rush (more about that in a while…).

In 1905, the Five Civilized Tribes proposed that Indian Territory become a state of the union in order to protect the natives' control of the land. The state was to be called Sequoyah after the Cherokee who created a system that made it possible to read and write in the Cherokee language. Had the proposal gone through, Sequoyah would have been the first state to have a Native American population majority. After the US government rejected the idea, two of the tribes' representatives, William Murray of the Chickasaw and Charles Haskell of the Creek, further proposed that the territories combine to be named Oklahoma. This time President Roosevelt signed the proclamation and Oklahoma became the 46th state.

We had arranged to meet up with my older daughter in Oklahoma. She likes to escape the British winters and her favourite destination is Central America, and who can blame her? She and a friend were on the way back from Costa Rica, via a road trip of their own up to California, stopping at the national parks on the way. As chance would have it, we were due to be in the west south central region at the same time, so we arranged to meet in Oklahoma. Also joining us were a couple of Oklahoman friends we had made a few of years previously, who live a about a two hour drive south of Oklahoma City. So just for the day there was a little gang of us. We all arranged to meet up at our hotel and they took us on a tour of the city.

On 22 April 1889, an estimated 50,000 people lined up to take part in the Land Rush (remember the Organic Act?). It was here that many of the cities and towns of Oklahoma were born. Any one settler was allowed to claim up to 160 acres, provided he lived there and improved the land. At noon a canon fired and away they went, galloping on their horses to claim their bit of land. This is why Oklahoma is littered with places that are just people's names, such as Edmund, Cameron, Enid and Norman.

Situated in Bricktown, Oklahoma City, the memorial to the Land Rush (interestingly called The Land Run rather than Land Rush) is beautiful. Forty-seven statues cast in bronze portray settlers, horses and wagons, with a dog and jackrabbit thrown in. Honestly, it is a brilliant piece of work. It really captures the moment. Each of the statues is different and to stand in amongst them you really get the sense that you are joining in and on the way to claim your own piece of land. In fact, it could be that I was actually there amongst them. I mean, I wasn't, but it seems that some time in the future I will invent time travel and take myself back to the Land Rush, so I was there. But wasn't yet. The reason for my confusing hypothesis is that there is a Nick Brown Creek in Oklahoma. There is, there really is! It's in Latimer County and is about 130 miles from Tulsa. Unfortunately it was too far away from our route to visit.

After the history and culture of the Land Run Memorial, we headed further into town to visit the Oklahoma City National Memorial. This was erected on the site of the Alfred P Murrah Federal Building which was destroyed in a bomb blast on 19 April 1995, just as the workers were arriving for their day's work. Up until 9/11, the Oklahoma City bombing was the deadliest act of terrorism ever carried out within the United States. As tends to be the case, the Memorial was eerily quiet and strangely peaceful. There is an archway at either end, one with 9:01 on and the other with 9:03 on – the last minute of peace and the first minute of recovery. Between the arches there is a reflecting pool. Only a few inches deep, the water runs across a black granite base, allowing visitors to see reflections of themselves. Along the side of the pool there are 168 empty chairs crafted from glass, bronze and stone, one for each victim. The Memorial is actually really tastefully done.

We headed back to our hotel, grabbed a bite to eat in a restaurant just across the street and bid each other a fond farewell. It was now that we got the only bit of rain in our entire trip. When I say a bit of rain, though, what I mean is that it absolutely hammered it down. Fortunately, we had just arrived back at the hotel and were able to watch the downpour from the window. For about 10 minutes the sky was dark and the noise of the rain was tremendous, like the horses that had taken part in the Land Rush were galloping past our window. And then, all of a sudden, it stopped again. The sky cleared and our mini monsoon was over. Half an hour later the streets were dry again and it was as if it had never happened.

About 80 miles from the Oklahoma – Texas border is the city of Clinton. We stopped here to visit the Oklahoma Route 66 Museum. As you walk round you come to various displays of 1950s style diners, some vintage cars and various pieces of Americana. What's really interesting, though, is a Dust Bowl display.

June to August 1936 saw one of the most severe heat waves in American history. By the end of June, record high temperatures had been set in many states including Kentucky, Arkansas, Mississippi and Missouri, all registering around the 112 degree Fahrenheit mark. But that was just for starters. July got hotter and August even more so. Even at nights certain states were measuring temperatures into the 80s. The country had seen nothing like it before, nor has it seen anything like it since. Just take a look at some of these recorded temperatures…

Mississippi : 111 degrees

Louisiana : 114 degrees

Texas : 120 degrees

Oklahoma : 120 degrees

Arizona : 123 degrees

California : 126 degrees

Even in the far north record high temperatures were being recorded...

Washington : 111 degrees

Montana : 113 degrees

North Dakota : 121 degrees

(For those who use the Celsius scale rather than Fahrenheit, 100 F = 37 C)

It was the same throughout the entire country. In fact, the only states not to hit the hundred mark were Vermont with 97, Maine with 96 and Rhode Island with a positively chilly 94. And don't forget, this was when air conditioning was still being developed and therefore wasn't widely available for use in homes! It must have been an absolute nightmare to live through and, in fact, many people didn't live through it. It is estimated that over 5,000 people lost their lives and, of course, it played havoc with crops and farming. And just to really rub it in, the previous winter had been one of the coldest on record. In February of that year, the average national temperature was just 26 degrees Fahrenheit, -3 Celsius.

Severe dust storms created what came to be known as the Dust Bowl. These storms were so bad that the sky was often turned to darkness. These dusty blizzards swept across the country, often reducing visibility to as little as six feet or even less. The Dust Bowl's biggest victims were the panhandle of Texas and Oklahoma, with adjoining parts of New Mexico, Kansas and Colorado also suffering. Thousands upon thousands of poverty-stricken families were forced to abandon their land or lost their homes entirely due to the ferocious storms. Many migrated west, principally towards California, in search of a new start. Unfortunately, they only found that the great depression of the 1930s had also affected their chosen destinations, and they were hardly any better off than they were in the places they had left behind. After the great depression ended, many headed back home, whilst others stayed where their families had settled.

The journey west was, of course, not what you would call an easy one to undertake. Migrants had to journey through extremely hazardous conditions and medical supplies amounted to as much as you could fit in your travel bag. Disease was not uncommon and, sadly, many didn't make it at all.

Heading out of Oklahoma into Texas, somewhere between the towns of Erick and Texola, the old 66 once again turned into not much more than a pathway, full of cracks and little tufts of grass shooting through. The I-40 wasn't too far away, but far enough for us to neither see nor hear it. Once we were away from the town of Texola we were back cutting through prairie land, again the only car on the road. In fact, so long had it been since we had seen any other vehicles, there were no concerns about just stopping to get out to stretch our legs at the state line.

Texola is one of those places in America whose name is basically just an amalgamation of the states it straddles, it this case Texas and Oklahoma. Yes, I realise that technically it should be Texoma, but there already is one of those 280-odd miles along the state line. At first I thought that this lacked imagination but when thinking about it, I changed my mind. It might not work in Britain because there are only two borders – England and Scotland being one, England and Wales being the other. A place called Engscot or Engwale would just sound stupid. In a country as big America, though, it does make sense, especially because there is so much open space. You can easily get lost whilst driving in the wilds and state portmanteau words are really quite handy. Some other examples are Calexico (California and New Mexico), Wycolo (Wyoming and Colorado), Marydel (Maryland and Delaware) and even a treble in Kentenia (Kentucky, Tennessee and Virginia). Brilliant!

Amarillo, Texas

"Is this the way to Amarillo?" asked Tony Christie. Well, sir, I can confirm that yes, it is. All you need to do is leave Oklahoma City, follow Route 66 to the west and there you are.

The drive from OK to TX was a really pleasant one. 250 miles of not much at all. Occasionally there was a little town to go through, but that was pretty much it. The open road, our Route 66 soundtrack in the CD player, fields as far as you can see, barely any other traffic at all and a beautiful hot sunny day. What more could you want? Occasionally we'd go past a ranch and see some cowboys doing their stuff but, for the most part, we didn't see anyone else at all. Which was great!

Amarillo came about when Mr J.I. Berry chose the location due to the railway passing through. His plan was to make it the region's main trading centre, and it became a cattle marketing centre. Originally, the settlement was named Oneida but was later changed to Amarillo due to the abundance of yellow wildflowers that grew there ('amarillo' being the Spanish word for 'yellow'). The population grew steadily and, aside for the cattle market, the city became known for its mills and storehouses.

After the first world war, industry grew in Amarillo. Natural gas and oil were also discovered in the area and the companies moved in. One particular gas field – the Cliffside – contained an unusually high amount of helium, leading to the establishment of the United States Helium Plant, and Amarillo became the world's biggest producer of helium.

Amarillo is also home of the Big Texan Steak Ranch. The ranch is actually a motel and steakhouse, and it is the eatery that has gained the Ranch it's fame. Painted bright yellow with a huge statue of a bull outside, the restaurant boasts that it is 'world famous for steaks'. The thing is, during our journey, we had seen many things that say they are world famous but, in most of their cases, their fame, I suggest, extends not much further than their own neighbourhood. However, the Big Texan Steak Ranch can genuinely make the claim.

If you are in the area and feel hungry – and I mean *hungry* – then this is the place for you. The Ranch is known as the place that sells the 72 ounce steaks. Yes, 72 ounces. It wasn't a typo. Just to put this into perspective, when we go out to a restaurant in Britain, the steaks offered would normally be 8 or 10 ounces and perhaps a 16 ouncer. This would normally, not always of course, but normally elicit a conversation along the lines of…

Man:	"Ooo, look at that, I'll have the 16 ounce steak."
Wife:	"You sure, that's a lot of meat…"
Man:	"Oh yeah, I like a steak."
Wife:	"Well, ok, if you're sure you'll eat it."

Man:	"But having said that, though, the chicken fillets in a creamy mushroom sauce sound nice."
Wife:	"They do, but we can always have that at home. Have the steak if you want the steak."
Man:	"Oh no, they do burgers too. Look at that one – a half pound burger with cheese, bacon and onion rings. Comes with fried and salad."
Wife:	"Have whatever you want."
Man:	"Yeah. Oooo, it's a tough one. No, I haven't had a decent burger in a while, and it comes with barbecue sauce."
Wife:	"Have that then."
Man:	"But that steak…"
Wife:	"Look, just choose one, the waiter's coming over."
Waiter:	"What would you like, sir?"
Man:	"Oooooo, I'm not sure…"
Wife:	"Just choose one."
Man:	"Oh, ok, the cheeseburger with bacon and onion rings."
Waiter:	"Certainly, sir."

When the waiter leaves the table, the man will then say "I'll have the big steak next time, it did sound good," whilst actually thinking to himself "Phew, got away with that one!"

For the Big Texan Steak Ranch to sell slabs the size of 72 ounces, our British diner would have had to have said to the waiter "I'll have four and a half of your big steaks, please" and actually be serious. The steak is free to anyone who can eat the meal – steak and trimmings – in less than one hour. Now, to me, an hour seems quite a generous allotment of time but, considering so few people actually manage to do it, I guess it is a decent challenge. Those who manage to beat the challenge have their names recorded on the restaurant's wall of fame.

The challenge started in 1960 when Bob Lee, the restaurant's founder, held a competition amongst the cowboys working in the stockyards. That competition was to see who could eat the most steak in one hour, the prize for the winner being $5. One cowboy managed to put away four one and a half pound steaks as well as sides. Mr Lee was so impressed that he declared it would be given free to anyone managing to consume the same amount again. The challenge takes place on a raised platform in the middle of the restaurant so the other diners can offer their support. At the time of writing, the record for completing the meal is held by Molly Schuyler, a competitive eater from Sacramento, California. She managed to polish it off in, wait for it, four minutes and 18 seconds! Yeah, just read that again … four minutes and 18 seconds. Seriously, that's just enough time to boil an egg! And in case you're wondering what the whole meal is, sides included, the menu reads 72 ounce steak, a baked potato, a shrimp cocktail, salad and a buttered roll.

No, I didn't.

On the outskirts of Amarillo is one of the most bizarre yet brilliant sights you will ever see. The Cadillac Ranch, situated right on the 66 herself, is an absolute must-see. Ten perfectly aligned Cadillacs in a field, covered in graffiti, half buried in the mud. Yes, that's right. Sounds weird, huh? Well, it is. But it's also fantastic.

In the 1970s, a local billionaire called Stanley Marsh wanted to create a piece of art that would both please and perplex. He contacted a group calling themselves The Ant Farm, and they put forward their design. Mr Marsh liked it and the Cadillac Ranch was born. The Ant Farm acquired 10 used Cadillacs and buried them nose down along the highway. Of course, it didn't take long for visitors to come and see the strange sight, some even graffitiing their own tags and messages on the cars. Others decided they would take their own personal souvenirs from the Cadillacs, smashing the windows to remove the radios and speakers and some even lost their doors. The wheels were welded to the axels to prevent them from disappearing as well. This may well have cheesed some people off, but Stanley Marsh went with it as an organic piece of art.

The Cadillac Ranch was exhumed in 1997 as the city limits of Amarillo were growing and Mr Marsh didn't want the Ranch eaten up by the ever expanding city. He had the Cadillacs replanted a few miles west and even collected the trash from the first sight to scatter in the new location! He encouraged visitors to continue visiting the Ranch and also to keep covering the cars in graffiti.

"But that's vandalism," you may protest.

Actually, not so. It is all perfectly legitimate and it means that every time you go there its different.

We parked up on the frontage road and took the pathway up to the Cadillacs. They were absolutely covered in graffiti with cans of spray paint dotted around on the ground. Not an inch of any of the cars was left uncovered. The reds, blues, yellows, greens, etc, that had been painted onto the cars glistened as the sun shone down and it was an amazing thing to see. We didn't have any spray paint with us so we couldn't add our own monikers, but plenty of pictorial evidence of our visit was taken. The Cadillac Ranch is absolutely one of the must-see attractions along Route 66.

Whilst in Amarillo, our stay for the night was at the Hilton Garden Inn. A very pleasant hotel with comfortable rooms. Well, I can't speak for anyone else's room, obviously, but our one was such and I can't imagine we were given the only comfortable room in the entire hotel. After a nice breakfast from the buffet, we returned to our room to collect our stuff and be on our way. We decided to use the elevator rather than walk up the stairs – well, why wouldn't you? – and when the door opened there were a couple of biker types inside. You know the sort – long grey goatie beards, bandanas on their heads, t-shirts and jeans. We stepped aside to let them out first in that typically polite British way of ours, exchanged greetings and a conversation ensued along the lines of…

"Heeyyy, you guys are British."

"Indeed we are."

"What brings you to Amarillo?"

"We're doing Route 66."

"Awesome. We did it a couple of years ago. It's great, isn't it?"

"It's been brilliant so far."

Another biker type appeared from the breakfast room, apparently another of their party.

"These guys are doing the route."

"Awesome."

"Have fun, guys."

And with that we parted, we into the elevator, they out to enjoy their day.

A pleasant and innocent enough meeting, but it got me thinking. You see, each time they said the word 'route' they pronounced it as 'rowt' whereas we say 'root'. To us, when anyone says 'rowt' it is spelt 'rout' and means a big defeat in a sports match or in a war. For example, 'the general's troops were routed' or 'it was a rout – five goals to nil'. Britain and America share a language, which is hardly surprising when you consider that it was the British who colonised the 'new world', but there are so many differences. Not massive differences, and nothing that you can't have a good guess at, but differences none-the-less. For example, in regaling you with the above story about meeting our biker friends, I twice used the word 'elevator' instead of the English 'lift'. Both are accurate by definition. An elevator elevates you to another floor and a lift lifts you to another floor (notice I'm not saying storey). So why the difference?

Also, our new best friends said that it was 'awesome' that we were doing the 'rowt'. The English definition of 'awesome' is apparently a little more grandiose than the American. 'Awesome' is defined as something breath-taking or that which inspires a feeling of reverence, and also something invoking fear. An atomic bomb may have awesome power or the Grand Canyon may be an awesome sight. In America, though, it seems that everything is awesome….

Me:	"I'll have the Philly Cheese Steak, please."
Waiter:	"Awesome."
Me:	"I'll meet you at 7:30."
My friend:	"Awesome."
Me:	"We're doing Route 66."
Biker Guy:	"Awesome."

I mean, it may be that Americans generally are breath-taken by pretty much everything and, if so, then I am genuinely envious of you. To continually have that feeling of breath-struckedness (that's not a word we use, I just made that one up) must be fantastic. Every day is a whole new adventure of discovery. It must be, well, awesome. It's like continually doing an excited little jump into the air, a couple of quick flat-handed claps with your eyes wide in disbelief and saying "yay". We Brits, of course, would rather nod appreciatively and say something like "jolly good" or "I'm pleased for you."

One thing I do like about American English is the logicality and descriptiveness of some words. Unlike us Brits, Americans don't walk along the pavement, they use the sidewalk. The word 'pavement' comes from the Latin 'pavimentum' which was a floor made of trodden down stones. 'Sidewalk', though? I mean how logical and obvious is that? Its bordering on genius. You can just imagine the conversation that took place between the construction workers who were first tasked with giving pedestrians a safe place to walk where they could be without fear of being run over by a car (although, having recently seen reruns of 'Starsky And Hutch', that's still no guarantee that you won't get mown down)…

Hank: "Well, that's the walkers-along-the-street-safety-mechanism laid."

Mack: "Awesome. I really think we should call it something else, though."

Hank: "Why? What's wrong with walkers-along-the-street-safety-mechanism?"

Mack: "It's not very snappy, is it? If I spot anyone veering of the road towards my wife and I, by the time I've shouted "Hey, Myrtle, you be

	careful on that walkers-along-the-street-safety-mechanism, there's a car heading right for you" it'll be too late."
Hank:	"You've got a point. What would you suggest, then?"
Mack:	"Well, let's think about this. It's where you walk along the side of the road…"
Hank:	"…Yeah. Tricky, huh…?"
Mack:	"Let's hope we don't have to find a name for the thing that enables us to walk across the road as well…"

And so the sidewalk and crosswalk were born.

Where this logic does fall down, though, is when you may wish to, how can I say this delicately, spend a penny. Is that a phrase Americans use? If somebody asked me if they could use my bathroom, I would assume they wanted to submerge themselves in my bathtub to rid themselves of some unwanted dirt or grime. I would expect to hear the sound of running water from a tap (or faucet), a bit of splishing and slashing and then frantic shouts of "oh no, I forgot to take in a towel". Even less logical than that, though, is 'restroom'. Surely a 'restroom' is a room where you would go for a rest, is it not? Perhaps there would be some nice comfy chairs, a few magazines to flick through, a coffee machine. I might even offer to come in with you. Imagine my horror if I did decide to follow you in…! No, I'm sorry, 'bathroom' and 'restroom' just won't do.

On top of this, there are many words common to both languages that mean different things. One obvious example is the word 'football'. To Brits, 'football' is a game where the protagonists will use their feet in order to move the small round object known as the 'ball' into their opponents' goal. To Americans, 'football' is a game where the protagonists will use their hands in order to move the small prolate spheroid object known as the 'ball' over their opponents' goal line. Will somebody please explain to me why the American game of 'football' is called 'football'? At no point do they use their feet aside from when attempting a field goal. Just that. That's it. It's the equivalent of calling British 'football' 'handball'. Unless he is the goalkeeper, the only time a footballer would use his hands legally is when taking a throw-in to restart the game after the ball has gone out of play.

Where it does start to get really confusing is when comparing items of clothing. Depending on whether you buy your outfit in Britain or America hinges on what exactly you will purchase and how daft you will end up looking. Let's say I'm in New York and I visit a clothing emporium. I tell the shop assistant that I am there to purchase pants, suspenders and a vest. They look at me with a smile, say "no problem, sir" and off they go to put together a nice outfit for me. Now let's say I'm in London and I visit a clothing emporium. I tell the shop assistant that I am there to purchase pants, suspenders and a vest. They look at me suspiciously, say "that's a most unusual outfit, sir, I presume this is just for private viewing" and off they go to put together an outfit that would only be seen in certain clubs I have no wish to frequent.

You see, what I have just purchased in London is the equivalent of what Americans would call underpants, a garter belt and an undershirt. What I should have asked for is trousers, braces and a waistcoat. That way I would get the same outfit as I would in New York and spare myself the indignity of having the outfitters' staff sniggering at me, telling their families all about me and eventually having the whole city look at me questionably and moving aside whenever we approached each other along the pavement / sidewalk / pedestrian crossing / crosswalk / ring road / beltway / lift / elevator / toilet / restroom / retail park / power center / shopping arcade / strip mall / underground / subway / whatever.

There are so many of these instances. I must qualify this by saying I don't mean there are so many instances of when normal law abiding citizens have to avoid me because I am some kind of freak, I mean so many instances of the language being the same but different.
Yay. Awesome.

Albuquerque, New Mexico

I must admit, I knew next to nothing about Albuquerque. In fact, what I knew about Albuquerque can be summed up in three sentences…

- It is in New Mexico
- It is mentioned in the chorus of the song 'The King Of Rock And Roll' by the British pop group Prefab Sprout
- It is difficult to spell

As I said … next to nothing.

Strangely enough, and in that bizarre way of mine, it's actually because of these three points that Albuquerque is one of those places that I've always wanted to visit, just to see what it's like.

New Mexico has long been on my 'need to go to' list. This is because I have always liked history and find the whole California / Texas / Mexico territory struggle from the 1800s quite fascinating. This is quite possibly because I used to love watching the old black and white TV series of Zorro that originally began in 1957. I have to say at this point that I'm not so old as to remember the original run. I used to watch it as a kid in the late 70s / early 80s. I loved all the swash-buckle and leaping from the roofs of burning buildings onto the back of a horse who would then stand up on his two hind legs as Zorro would point his sword at the sky before replacing it in its sheaf, ruffling the hair of the local raggedly dressed urchins and waving his hat at the cheering crowd before galloping off over the hills.

The Prefab Sprout song is one of those songs from my younger years that just makes me smile. Whenever I hear it, it transports me back to 1988. I was 16 at the time, just leaving school, carefree and the world was my oyster. I was working at a local radio station and it was just a brilliant period of my life. I always look back at 1988 as one of the great years for music – the disco sound of the late 70s / early 80s had become a lot more sophisticated, the experimentation with the new music technologies was producing so much fresh and exciting stuff and dance music was just starting to merge into the mainstream with the advent of House Music. The pop scene was absolutely buzzing and producing great track after great track and such luminaries as Michael Jackson, Madonna and Prince were in their pomp. At the same time, there was also a re-emergence of the more rocky sound that had begun to die out as the 70s ended. Oooo, I've gone all misty eyed…!

Anyway, 'The King Of Rock And Roll' was one of those songs that was just perfect for its time. "Hot dog, jumping frog, Albuquerque" went the chorus, sung in an almost wistful way, befitting of a song delivered from the point of view of an old rocker who is desperately trying to still be popular and important even though his best years are past him. A great song!

And the spelling? Well, basically its just a funny word, isn't it, Albuquerque?

Albuquerque.

Just say it six or seven times and it sounds really silly. As if Albuquerque is a real place! It sounds almost as daft as that Saskatchewan that the Canadians have been pretending is one of their provinces.

I had always pictured Albuquerque as a bit of a wild west sort of place out in the desert full of cactus plants. The sort of place where people wore ponchos and sombreros and had three days worth of stubble. The sort of place where I'd push open the small wooden door of the local saloon and just stand there looking slowly around. Everything has gone quiet and all eyes are on me as I saunter over to the bar. The only sound is the flapping of the doors until they come to a rest and the creek of the floorboards as I walk slowly across the room. I look over to the wizened old men in the corner playing dominoes and nod a greeting. They just stare back. I turn to the bartender and say a single word – "Whiskey" – in a husky whisper. Without breaking eye contact he pours me a whiskey and I down it in one before replacing the glass back on the counter. An awkward few seconds pass before the bartender breaks into a hearty laugh and says "Welcome, stranger". It's as if he has uttered the magic words and the saloon kicks back into life again. All conversation restarts as if it had never been put on pause, the old men start knocking their dominoes on the old wooden table and someone I've never seen before pulls up a stool and asks what brings me to town.

As it turns out, the wild west image isn't a million miles away. Ok, it isn't actually still a cowboy town, but the almost 300 mile drive from Amarillo to Albuquerque produces miles and miles of absolute nothingness. And when I say nothingness, I mean nothingness. As far as the eye can see there is just grass desert in all directions. Now that might sound boring but, actually, it has it's own charm – it's amazing that you can drive for four and a half hours and see nothing at all.

To say there is absolutely nothing is perhaps a little harsh on the towns of Vega, Adrian, San Jon and Moriarty but, to be fair, they do verge on belonging to the 'blink and you miss them' category.
"Hey look, there's a couple of houses coming up."
"So there is. Maybe we can stop for while and have a look around."
"Oh no, sorry, we've just gone through."
Hardly time to get from 'hot dog' to 'jumping frog'…!

One place we did stop was at Glenrio, right on the Texas – New Mexico border. We parked up, nipped in to the café and had a chat with the locals. Well, we would have had we gone back in time to the early 1950s. Glenrio was never what you'd call a big place – 50 people there at any one time would have been a game of sardines – but a travellers' stop it was. The state border runs right by what is the remains of a motel and café. In fact, the motel used to advertise itself as 'The last motel in Texas' or 'The first motel in Texas' depending from which way you were approaching it.

Glenrio was once part of the Ozark Trail, a series of locally maintained roads running from St Louis to Santa Fe. These roads were defunct when Route 66 came about. It's location right on the border led to some cunning business practices. For example, the gas station was built on the Texas side of the state line due to New Mexico's higher taxes. On the other side of the coin, New Mexico was home to the bar and motel due to that particular Texan county being, at the time, one of those where the government forbade the sale of alcoholic beverages.

By the late 1960s, most of the rural sections of the Route and been superseded by the I-40. The road between Glenrio and Tucumcari was one notable exception to this. Notable because, unfortunately, it became increasingly dangerous to the heavier traffic passing through and it picked up the rather charming nickname of Slaughter Lane due to the amount of accidents, many of which were fatal, that occurred on this particular stretch. Not unreasonably, the I-40 eventually bypassed Glenrio and it was this action that brought about it's death. Today it is a ghost town – barely even that – with four dilapidated and crumbling buildings and a gas station.

The bit of Route 66 that runs through it is nothing more than a dirt track. It is deserted and deadly silent but, because of it, was one of our highlights of the drive. We could get out of the car and just walk down the middle of the road without fear of being knocked down. The landscape was barren, just grassland as far as the eye could see. It's hard to imagine there was once a hospitality industry here, albeit a small one. Nowadays there is no way anybody would be on this road unless it was specifically to see Glenrio for what it is now – a relic of the past. And the only way this will ever change is if a big investor comes along and makes a tourist destination of it by either trying to rebuild the town as it was or by opening some cafés and restaurants and souvenir shops. I really hope this doesn't happen, and I don't think it will. Those remaining buildings will just slowly crumble over time and eventually there will be nothing left to see. Glenrio will be a mere footnote in the pages of the history books.

200 miles further on, we reached Albuquerque. The city was founded in 1706 by Senor Francisco Cuervo y Valdes who, at the time, was the Governor of New Mexico. It wasn't until the late 1700s, though, that a permanent population was established round the central plaza. This was because the homes were previously only being inhabited on Sundays due to the 'residents' working on their farms throughout the rest of the week.

The Mexican War of Independence saw Albuquerque, along with the rest of the state, given over to Mexico. This transfer was only short-lived, though, as the territory was retaken by American forces in the Mexican – American War in the 1840s, merely 20 years later.

When the Santa Fe railway reached Albuquerque in 1880, a new town was built and became a popular and important stop en route. This led to the Old Town entering a decline, as all the new businesses naturally wanted to be as close to the railway as possible. Even the courthouse was moved. In 1949, the Old Town was annexed by 'New' Albuquerque and some improvements were made, including the laying of paved streets, and ever since then the Old Town has been a popular destination for tourists. And we could see why.

Our hotel wasn't far from Old Town, so we mosied on down to have a look round and we really liked it. It isn't what you'd call a lively place, but it was really nice. It is exactly how you would imagine an old Wild West town would have looked, with bars, trading posts and eateries snaking round the town square, with a few art galleries thrown in. The shops were full of local Navajo, Pueblo and Apache products, including etchings, carvings and blankets. No-one seemed to be in a hurry, everybody was just strolling about or sitting round the bandstand just watching the world go by.

We had some spare time before the next leg of our journey, so we decided to go up Sandia Mountain. When we got to the top, we were sure glad we did. Two miles above sea level, the views were astounding. The mountain rises above the Rio Grande Valley and you can see for miles, a bird's eye view of the state of New Mexico.

Those of you who hablas Espanol will probably be asking why it is called the Sandia Mountain, when 'sandia' means 'watermelon'. There are a couple of popular explanations, so choose whichever one you prefer. Firstly, it is thought to be a reference to the reddish colour of the range at sunset and, when viewed from the west, there is a thin green line of conifer trees near the top, looking like the watermelon's rind. The second possible explanation is that the Spaniards called it Sandia in the 1540s because they thought the squash gourd plants that grow there were actually watermelons.

Searching what else to do on the all-knowing world-wide-web, we discovered a vineyard called Casa Rodena, so we decided to do a bit of wine tasting. At $10 a go, sampling five different wines, that struck us as a decent price. When we arrived, there was a parking attendant at the gate welcoming us into a heaving car park. We wondered if the Casa was always this busy as we strolled up the pathway into the main house. When we got there, it turned out that there was a posh luncheon being served as, unbeknown to us, it was Mothers' Day. So there we were, in our t-shirts, shorts, baseball caps and London accents, bowling right into a fancy soiree full of smartly dressed families and winery members who were professionally sampling the product of the vine, sniffing, swirling, sipping, taking special note of the colouration and commenting on the lingering feeling in their mouths and how the tannins of each sample were leaving their taste buds tingling and seducing them into more. We, on the other hand, tried each sample, rated them on our special scale of 'that one's alright' to 'yeah, I quite like that' before wondering whether or not their café sold the local beer...!

(Actually, it was really enjoyable and the wines were good. Not only that, but because it was a special event, the price was halved so we got to taste for $5 each instead of $10, so that was a bonus!)

The route out of Albuquerque into Arizona was once again a mixture of wilderness and highway. For long sections we seemed to be the only people on Earth, only to then be directed back onto the I-40 for a while before coming off again into the barren grassy desert on roads full of cracks. Every so often along the route there would be an Indian trading post but precious little else.

Batman and Robin with the Batmobile. Or, if you prefer, me and Alex with our Dodge Challenger at the start of the route. Roy Rogers had Trigger, the Lone Ranger had Silver, but our trusty steed had over 300 horsepower!

Gulp! That's our hotel just across the way, in Springfield, Illinois.

The man who invented rock 'n' roll. Chuck Berry, that is, not me!
His statue is on the Delmar Loop, St Louis.

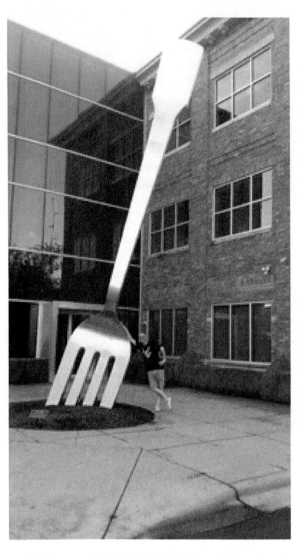

The world's biggest fork, Springfield, Missouri. Just imagine the size of that steak...

The Land Rush Monument in Oklahoma. Well, a small piece of it, anyway. It is a beautiful piece of art.

Along the route there were a few things that made us think "Why would you do that?". The Cadillac Ranch in Amarillo is the perfect example. The answer, of course, is "Because I can and it's brilliant!"

All that's left of Glenrio.
Above : The first or last motel in Texas, depending on which way
you approach it from.
Below : The gas station that was once filled many a car.

Holbrook, Arizona

Here's a question for you ... how big is America? Go on, guess. No? Ok, I'll tell you. It's roughly 3,700,000 square miles, give or take one or two. That's quite a size, I think you'll agree. In fact, the only countries in the world that are bigger are Russian and Canada. That being the case, what do you think are the chances of accidentally bumping into your daughter? Without going too much into the actual figures and percentages and clever mathematical stuff, the chances are rated at what I believe it officially termed 'quite substantial'.

Just as we were approaching the New Mexico – Arizona border, my daughter (remember her from Oklahoma?) sent a picture of the 'Welcome To Arizona' state sign. It turns out they were about 20 minutes in front of us! A couple of hurried messages later we arranged to meet up at the Petrified Forest National Park, which Route 66 cuts through.

Thus named due to the large amount of petrified wood and fallen trees, the Petrified Forest has an area of about 345 square miles and straddles the border between Apache County and Navajo County. It was established as a national park in 1962 with 146 square miles of land but additional land parcels have been acquired over time. The northern part of the park – the bit that we explored – lay within the Painted Desert, a region in the 'four corners' area of Arizona, New Mexico, Colorado and Utah (if you look at a map of the USA, those four states are slotted together, their corners touching).

The phrase 'it has to be seen to be believed' is over used these days – television adverts tell us the local furniture shop's sale has to be seen to be believed, your friend's new hairstyle has to be seen to be believed (you can take that either way) – but whoever it was that first uttered those immortal words, I wouldn't be surprised if they were here when they said it. I can describe the varying colours in the sand and rocks in many ways … a depiction of each season, perhaps, with the dusty reds of a scorching summer sun, the greens of newly regenerated spring trees by well watered streams, the yellows and browns of fallen Autumn (Fall) leaves, the ghostly silvers of a frosty winter day; some may call it God's paintbox; or what about an award winning layered cake? None of these, however, do it justice. It has to be seen to be believed. It is just stunningly beautiful.

The four of us drove through the forest and up to the desert. There are lots of places to stop and take a walk and just be amazed at the scenery. It's like the landscape of an uninhabited alien planet. Miles and miles of rocky terrain and parched grass, with every so often what was presumably a fallen tree looking so old that it would crumble as soon as you touch it. It was then back to the visitors' centre where their car is parked, we said our good-byes (again) and headed off in our different directions – they towards Yosemite and us back along Route 66.

Holbrook, our next stop, is only 20 miles from the Petrified Forest. Formed in 1881 and named after Henry Holbrook, the first chief engineer of the Atlantic And Pacific Railroad, the community sprang up when it became the headquarters of the Aztec Land And Cattle Company who had purchase a million acres of land in northern Arizona. Cowboys were hired, many of whom were wanted and hiding from arrest. Cattle and horse rustling became commonplace and, almost inevitably, various conflicts broke out, with Holbrook seeing its fair share of action. The Blevins family were notorious rustlers and were also known for taking no nonsense and dealing with anyone who stood in their way. When the sheriff of Apache County, Commodore Perry Owens, discovered the whereabouts of the Blevins' house in Holbrook, he rode over to serve a warrant for their arrest. As you can imagine, they didn't exactly say "yes of course, sheriff, we didn't wish to cause you any trouble" and Commodore Owens was fired at. A shoot-out ensued. In less that a minute three lay dead with others injured. Owens became somewhat of a local legend and his shootings were ruled as self-defence.

Another notorious episode in Holbrook's history took place in Terrill's Cottage Saloon in 1886. As it seemed to be the way in wild west saloons, cowboys would drink, play poker and have a fight. One particular encounter, though, got somewhat out of hand. A disagreement broke out over the poker game but, not content with a bout of fisticuffs or, Heaven forbid, talking the whole thing out like gentlemen, gun shots were fired. It's reckoned that as many as 26 people may have died in the shoot-out, the population of the town at the time being only 250! Written records say that the saloon floor was awash with 'buckets of blood'. From then on, Terrill's Cottage Saloon became known as the Bucket Of Blood Saloon and the section of Central Avenue where the saloon stands is known as Bucket Of Blood Street. The saloon is still there as a monument to Holbrook's colourful past, boarded up but nonetheless an absolute must for any visitor.

And people wonder why it was that Holbrook became known as 'the town too tough for women and churches'…

After spending the night in Holbrook and somehow managing not to get involved in a shoot-out or becoming the victims of car rustlers, our next stop was Flagstaff. Pretty much all the way there the 66 dissected arid grassland until the out of town service stations and motels told us we were nearing our destination. Once in Flagstaff, before checking in to our hotel and exploring, we indulged ourselves in a detour north along the 180 up to the Grand Canyon. Well, why wouldn't you? We can't come all this way and be so close without doing so, can we? That would be like going to Paris and not bothering to see the Eiffel Tower, or going to Sydney and giving the Opera House a miss, or going to San Francisco and finding some other way to cross the bay other than the Golden Gate Bridge.

*

So, the Grand Canyon, then. Well, what can I say? Its just a hole in the ground.

Well, technically, I suppose so, yes, but it isn't not your average pothole though, is it? The Grand Canyon is 277 miles long, gets up to 18 miles wide and plummets over 6,000 feet. It is bigger in area than the state of Rhode Island, the smallest of the 50. It is also home to the Havasupai Indian Reservation who have been living there since way before it ever became a national park. The village is located right at the canyon's base and is inaccessible by road.

We parked up at the visitors' centre and got one of the buses that takes sightseers to the various vantage points around the canyon. There is a general hubbub of excitement and anticipation as the bus drives us to the first stop. We all file out and as soon as everybody walks down to the canyon's edge, the noise stops. There are a few seconds of silence as everybody tried to take in what they saw and then there is one collective "woooaaahhh". The next thing that happens is that everybody starts taking selfies as near as they dare to the edge without tumbling to their doom. Remember what I said about the Painted Dessert? That it has to be seen to be believed? Well, double the has-to-be-seen-to-be-believedness and you have something approaching what the Grand Canyon has to offer. Honestly, I cannot possibly write the words to accurately describe the shapes cut of the rock, the colours, the absolute vastness of it all. If you ever have the chance to go and visit the Grand Canyon please, please, please do so. Assuming you like looking at holes in the ground, that is…

Flagstaff, Arizona

After a really quite breathtaking morning at the Grand Canyon we head back towards Flagstaff. Can you guess what Flagstaff is named after? Think carefully, now. Any ideas? No? Well, ok then, I'll tell you. It's named after a flagstaff. There are any number of stories as to who was actually involved in making said pole, but the most popular suggests that it was erected by a party of lumberjacks who stripped a lone pine tree and nailed an American flag to it in celebration of the US centenary on 4 July 1876. Henceforth the settlement was then known as Flagstaff.

Flagstaff is often referred to as The City Of Seven Wonders because of its location in the Coconino National Forest and its location with regards to the Grand Canyon, Oak Creek Canyon, Walnut Canyon, the Wupatki National Monument, Sunset Crater and the San Francisco Peaks. We've already talked about the Grand Canyon and Oak Creek and Walnut Canyons are, as the names would suggest, other holes in the ground, the Coconino National Forest is a national forest, but what of the other three?

The Wupatki National Monument, 'Wupatki' meaning 'tall house' in the Hopi language, is a series of pueblos built by Native Americans during the 12th and 13th centuries. Altogether there are more than 800 ruins but only five are open to visitors.

Sunset Crater is a cinder cone dating back to the eleventh century. It gets its name because when the sun is setting the crater is illuminated. The eruption of the long extinct volcano created the cone which now rises 1,000 feet above the surrounding area.

The San Francisco Peaks is a volcanic mountain range. Named by Spanish friars after Saint Francis, it contains the six highest peaks in the state of Arizona. That being the case, if anyone ever asks you to visit the San Francisco Peaks don't, as you may initially be tempted, head towards the San Fran in Cali. That would mean you would be a 13 hour drive away from your intended destination assuming, of course, that you don't think they mean any of the 43 other San Franciscos in the Americas (there are 22 in Mexico alone!). But you wouldn't think that, would you? Surely not. For the record, the San Francisco Peaks were named almost 150 years before the Golden Gate City.

Flagstaff is also home to the Lowell Observatory. This, my friends, is no run of the mill observatory, oh no. The Lowell Observatory was founded by the astronomer Percival Lowell in 1894 and, a few years later, he started a project to find a ninth planet in our solar system, which he called Planet X. It is at this point I feel the need to interject. Brilliant as Mr Lowell was and much as I love and admire anything to do with space exploration, it is my humble opinion that he chose the wrong name here. Surely it should have been Planet IX, should it not? Would Planet X give the impression that there were already another nine known planets and he was looking for the tenth? It's like coming up with a recipe for 9 UP to supersede its predecessor.

Interjection over.

Mr Lowell devoted a fair amount of his time to finding his new planet but, sadly, upon his death in 1916, to no avail. Or so he thought. Unbeknownst to him, he had actually captured a couple of images of a new planetary body but they weren't recognized for what they actually were. It wasn't until 13 March 1930 that Planet X was officially discovered and the Observatory also had the honour of giving it a name and Pluto was chosen after the Greek god of the underworld, also known as Hades. For those not up to speed on Greek mythology, Pluto or Hades was part of a trinity of gods along with Zeus, the god of the sky, and Poseidon, the god of the sea. Interestingly enough, Pluto the dog also made his first appearance in 1930 in the Mickey Mouse film 'Chain Gang'.

The Lowell Observatory was also used to map the moon for the lunar explorations of the Apollo space programme in the 1960s and early 70s.

When Route 66 was aligned through Flagstaff, the Santa Fe Railroad also opened a new depot there, initially to combat what they foresaw as a change of ways of doing things. Previously it was they who had controlled the ins and outs of the town and didn't really want this new road taking their customers. The locals, anticipating, a rise in the tourist market, also clubbed together to fund a new hotel for the town, the Hotel Monte Vista, which opened on new year's day 1927. The hotel is there to this day and, during the 1940s and 50s, was a regular haunt for Hollywood stars who would often be filming in nearby locations. The hotel's guestbook includes such as Bing Crosby, Bob Hope and Esther Williams. The following year, 1928, Flagstaff was incorporated as a city and from then on has become a popular stop for those travelling down the Mother Road.

Another thing we had noticed all through our trip was the difference in politeness and what is socially acceptable to Brits and Americans. Everywhere we went, people would speak to us and say hello and, not only that, but seem to be genuinely interested in us. I've decided to write about this now as it has been the same right from Chicago and I have no reason to suspect that California will be any different, particularly considering the amount of tourists that flock to the Californian sun.

I've mentioned a couple of times that in certain places we got into conversations with people we had obviously never met before and will more than likely never see again. In this regard America beats Britain hands down. At pretty much every stop, be it overnight or at something interesting along the route, there was somebody that we spoke with. It would normally be along the lines of why we were there and what we were doing along the route, sometimes they would be offering little bits of advice on what to see or they will extolling the virtues of their favourite bits of the country. To be honest, it made a nice change. In Britain, or at least in England, this doesn't tend to happen very much. Obviously, there are those who will say hello but, in the main, that's as far as it goes. As a nation of people, we are just more guarded. We don't like giving too much away and I don't really know why that should be. Do we think that any piece of information we give out will somehow be used illicitly against us? Just to underline what I mean, I feel that I need to provide a bit of a translation service, what Americans would say compared with what the English would say…

American: "Hi there, how are you guys doing?"

English: "All right?"

American: "You're doing Route 66? That's awesome, you'll really enjoy it. What a great thing to do, America's main street."

English: "Nice one."

American: "Sorry, guys, but I really need to get off now. It's been great talking with you. I hope you enjoy your time here in the States. Do come back again, won't you? Hey, if you're ever in *(names home state)* be sure to look me up."

English: "See ya."

What is also in stark contrast is how pleased people are to see you, and this is particularly evident in the hospitality industry. In every restaurant or hotel or bar or store that we went into on the route we were treated like customers rather than inconveniences. We would be given cheery smiles, conversation would ensue and they would make sure we were given the best experience their outlet could possibly offer. In some restaurants in England – not all, obviously, but an unfortunate amount – the impression is given that they would rather you hadn't turned up at all. How dare we interrupt their day! Didn't we know that they were texting their friends or trawling through social media? I mean, for goodness sake, it's as if they are there to provide us with a service! The waitress will appear at our table notepad in hand and say "Are you ready to order?" No hint of a 'hello' or 'how are you' or anything that might give us the mistaken view that we are customers and, actually, it's we upon whom their jobs depend. American waitresses will often make a little comment on our meal selections, something like 'yeah, good choice' or 'oh yeah, I'll often that myself' and seem like they mean it. In England you get to the end of the order and the waitress then grunts a 'right' and off she goes. And then when you're done and paying, the American waitress will say "Well, it's been a pleasure, we'd love to see you back some time, enjoy the rest of your day." The English waitress will say "At last, I was waiting for you to get out and give me some peace, you snivelling little worm, go on, clear off. And if you ever dare to come back I will personally slice you into little pieces with one of the chef's knives and feed you to the cat who, incidentally, I had let nibble your plates of food before bringing them out to you. So sue me!"

Public transport is another thing. I've ridden the subway during a previous trip to New York and, although the sort of conversations I talked about earlier didn't happen, people at least acknowledged us, sometimes with a smile, sometimes with a 'hi'. Also, if they weren't entirely sure, people would ask their fellow passengers where the train was heading and if it was calling at a particular station which, you have to say, is the obvious and sensible thing to do.

On the London Underground this is not the case. I'm not sure if it is actually illegal to acknowledge that there is anybody else in the carriage with you, but such a crime is treated as if it is. You have to try your very best to make sure you are the first one in when the doors open, even if it means having to turn sideways and slip in through the smallest crack rather than wait an extra two or three seconds for them to open fully. The next stage in the operation is to scan the area as quickly as is humanly possible and then walk very quickly – but not run, that would be too much of a giveaway – to the nearest free seat, preferably at the end of a row. You then flop down onto the seat and, at the speed of light, produce a newspaper or book to read. This serves two purposes. Firstly, it makes sure you don't see, even though you do, the poor little old lady who has limped on behind you and who looks like she could keel over at any moment. The problem here is that if she or any of the other passengers notice that you have in fact seen her, you would be obliged to give up your seat. Secondly, if you are staring at a page of print, you won't have to make eye contact with anybody else. This is singularly the most embarrassing thing that could ever happen. If you do accidentally make eye contact with somebody else, the normal procedure is to instantly look away and hope that such a disaster doesn't happen again. But if you accidentally make eye contact with a member of the opposite sex, well, that doesn't bear thinking about. There's that awkward moment of asking yourself if you should look away instantly, but if you do she might think you were looking at her covertly and then you might have a law suit to deal with or she might even say very loudly so everyone else could hear "are you looking at me?" This may well be worse than having a law suit to deal with because the whole carriage would look at you and you may well die of embarrassment. And if you're not entirely sure where the train was heading or if it was calling at a particular station, instead of asking someone you have to look at the map and try to work it out for yourself. This would often mean leaning right forward so you are almost falling off your seat. The downside here is that it will entice other people to look at you due to your eccentric display and then the whole eye contact controversy would start all over again. The other option is the obvious and sensible one – ask somebody. This, of course, is a total non-starter because everyone else would think you are a complete weirdo.

Kingman, Arizona

Half way between Flagstaff and Kingman we came to quite possibly the most bonkers piece of Route 66 along its entire course. And when I say 'bonkers' I also mean fantastic. Having driven for about 75 miles with nothing on either side of us, we came to a town called Seligman. What a place! How would you describe the main thoroughfare? Welcoming? Certainly. Brightly coloured? Absolutely. Tacky? Some might say but I love that sort of thing. Allow me to explain...

The Rusty Bolt and Bone Daddy's gift shops are single storey shops who share a roof. The roof in question also doubles as a balcony upon which sit a series of dummies. By dummies I mean shop window mannequin types. Apparently, these dummies change their appearance from time to time. When we rolled into town, sitting above Bone Daddy's were a couple of female mannequins in Route 66 t-shirts, one blue and one pink, and in the doorway of the shop was another in a silver mini dress.

Slightly further down the road is Delgadillo's Snow Cap. Underneath the giant wooden ice cream, the advertising board tells us it sells malts, creamy root beer and shakes, burritos and dead chicken! Well, to be honest, if I ordered a chicken meal I would hope the bird is dead. In fact, I would actually make that assumption. You see, I'm not in the habit of ordering a live chicken with fries and a shake! The Snow Cap also advertises cheeseburgers with cheese. Now this opens up a series of possibilities…

1. A cheeseburger.
2. A cheeseburger with extra cheese in it, although this would surely just be a cheeseburger as well, wouldn't it? I'm not an expert but I would imagine that what makes a cheeseburger a cheeseburger is that one of the main ingredients is cheese and not necessarily the amount of cheese. One slice or twenty slices, if it's inside the two halves of bun on top of – or underneath, I don't mind – a burger, then that's a cheeseburger.
3. A cheeseburger with an extra side of cheese on the side.

There are another couple of gift shops further down the road, both with vintage cars outside them and along the other side of the road there are a few motels, the Road Kill Saloon and a general store. The street is about a mile long and then that it is, back to nothingness again. Depending on your point of view, it's either fabulous or dreadful. I, for the record, side with the former. It is an absolutely perfect little stop along Route 66.

It could, though, have been an awful lot different if it wasn't for one Angel Delgadillo. He was born on the route in 1927 just when the new Chicago to Santa Monica road was coming about, and Route 66 seemed to somewhat take over his life. He followed in his father's footsteps by becoming a barber, and for this he attended the American Barber College in California, which just happened to be on their section of the 66. His apprenticeship was carried out in Williams, Arizona, also on the Mother Road. When he opened his own barber shop, he used the same building his father had used. Guess which road that was on…?

In 1972, he moved his barber shop to Seligman in order to take advantage of the adjustment in alignment of his favourite route. Of course, when the interstate was opened, the through traffic dried up somewhat and pretty much over night Seligman's industry fell on it's face. What also didn't help is the fact that only one single road sign alerted travellers that there was actually a place called Seligman. This didn't go down too well with Angel Delgadillo and he demanded a meeting with the officials responsible for the signage and succeeded in securing a further four mileage signs. Despite this, the traffic and therefore business was still sparse. Angel, though, was not prepared for Seligman to become a place of the past, another town killed by the interstate age.

Over the years he had heard many stories from those who would reminisce about the halcyon bygone days when Route 66 would bring a stream of travellers into town, and many stories from people who were amongst those visitors. It was these stories that convinced Angel the way forward was to look backwards. Route 66 obviously meant so much to so many people, so why was it not made a historic highway? He visited all the businesses along the route to Kingman to trump up support for his campaign. On

18 February 1987, he called a meeting for anyone who was interested and wanted to attend and the Historic Route 66 Association Of Arizona was founded. Interest grew and the call for Route 66 merchandise got louder and louder. A letter writing campaign throughout Arizona was organised and the stretch of Route 66 between Seligman and Kingman was indeed made 'Historic Route 66'. This was soon extended to the California border. On 23 April 1988, the Historic Route 66 Foundation Of Arizona held a 'fun car rally', with 153 vehicles taking part, with special events held along the route. It was indeed a big event as guests included Bobby Troupe, the writer of the song 'Get Your Kicks On Route 66', and music was provided by The Dick Clark Band. Will Rogers Jr, son of the actor Will Rogers, gave the dedication and Governor Rose Mofford cut the ribbon. The day was such a success that an annual event has been established.

Seligman is now an integral part of the Route 66 experience and Angel Delgadillo established it as such. He became somewhat of a celebrity and has appeared in newspapers, magazines and has had songs written about him. He is known as the Guardian Angel of Route 66 and even features in a Route 66 exhibition at the Smithsonian National Museum Of American History in Washington DC.

Angel Delgadillo take a bow – a true modern day American hero, a person who absolutely made a difference.

After the wonder of Seligman, upon reaching Kingman, it seemed to me – and I mean absolutely no disrespect when I say this – that we might have actually somehow managed to arrive 1970s. Driving into the town, there were lots of motels along the route with big multi-coloured signs, some advertising they had a coin-op laundry and cable tv whilst some were advertising colour tv and a phone in each room; there was a liquor store; a couple of burger bars; there was even a scrapyard. And no building seemed to be more than just a single storey high. I could just imagine the clientele rocking up in their Chevrolet Corvettes, Ford Mustangs and Pontiac Firebirds, driver's window down, Glen Campbell or Steely Dan playing in the tape deck, depending on taste. Most would, of course, be wearing a vest and blue jeans with a huge belt buckle, walrus moustaches and pilot sunglasses.

Don't get me wrong, I'm not mocking here, it was marvellous. This was the sort of place I was hoping we would drive through. Big cities are great and, obviously, the States has a fair amount of them, but I wanted to experience that contrast. I wanted to see places like those that I remember watching on tv when I was but a mere boy, before the days of easy and frequent long-haul flights, before the internet, before social media, when America seemed a world away and our entire picture of it was made from what we watched on the cop shows. The America where cars would skid round corners, their tyres screeching, crashing through boxes of fruit and veg that some poor store owner had been piling up, sending apples all over the road. The America where Burt

Reynolds would pull over at a gas station and immediately provoke the suspicion of the entire town for no decipherable reason other than he winked at the girl who served him as he turned back to look at her from the door before exiting, and then gave his Good Buddy Bulldog a 10-4 on his CB Radio before driving off with his muffler backfiring. And it was Kingman, more than anywhere else on the trip, that delivered that feeling. I almost convinced myself we would be flying home courtesy of Freddie Laker.

Our motel for the night was the Rodeway Inn, which was on Route 66 itself right in the heart of Kingman. When we got to our room there was a little tribute above the door to a previous guest. There was a framed 7-inch single called 'Hot Rod Lincoln' by Charlie Ryan with a picture of Mr Ryan. When I checked with the motel manager he confirmed that yes, Charlie Ryan did indeed stay in that very room. How exciting is that!? Not only did we stay in the same hotel as Elvis Pressley in Springfield, Missouri, but in the same room as Charlie Ryan in Kingman, Arizona! I have to apologise to Mr Ryan now, but neither myself nor Alex knew the song 'Hot Rod Lincoln' so, naturally, we looked it up. Written in 1955, it seems that the song is actually a reply to another song, 'Hot Rod Race' by Arkie Shibley. That song describes a race between two hot rods. The contest is neck and neck until another car overtakes them both, and it from this driver's perspective that 'Hot Rod Lincoln' is written.

In town, we had a look round the Kingman visitors' centre which included a Route 66 museum which was really interesting. It had old maps, cars, newspaper clippings, memorabilia and a film was continually running chronicling the history of the route.

The ticket for the museum also gave us access to the Mohave Museum which presents the history of north-western Arizona to its visitors. And here's an interesting fact ... the Mohave Museum has one of only three complete collections of presidential portraits in the whole of the United States. The other two are in the White House and the National Portrait Gallery. Not only that, but they also have portraits of all the First Ladies, too.

Just as a little side point, talking of First Ladies, try this little poser to test your friends at parties ... which two First Ladies were not born in the USA? The obvious one is Melania Trump, wife of Donald, who was born Melania Knavs in Novo Mesto, Slovenia, and the other is Louisa Adams, the wife of John Quincy Adams. She was born Louisa Johnson in London, England. And here's a little side point to the side point to amaze your chums even further ... there was one First Lady who wasn't married to a President. The woman in question was Harriet Lane, who was the niece of James Buchanan, but was still considered the First Lady. One word of warning when amazing your audience with this one, though. They might throw back to you the names of Andrew Jackson, Martin Van Buren, William Harrison, John Tyler and Chester Arthur and say that they weren't married yet had First

Ladies. If that is what happens then you can retort along the lines of "Well, my learned friend, you are both right and wrong. You are correct in saying they were not married, but incorrect in saying they had First Ladies. Their non-spousal female relatives were awarded the title of White House Hostesses, so Miss Lane remains the only non-wife to be First Lady."

Interesting, huh…!?

Just down the road from our motel was Denny's Diner, where we decided to take our evening meal. I like diners. They are everything that I want it a restaurant. They are friendly places, comfortable, bright and colourful, the walls are decorated with memorabilia, you don't have to dress up smart and they normally have a decent choice of food. I also like the way they not only have tables and booths, but stools along the food counters so that you can go in on your own and not feel like Billy No Mates when everywhere else there are families. You can grab a stool, order a burger and a beer and strike up a conversation with the person next to you and no-one would know you've never seen each other before, nor are you likely to again. Diners are generally pretty cheap, too. Some would say that reflects in the food but I disagree. I like diners and I will always defend them.

Casting our eyes down the menu we noticed that a few of the dishes were advertised as having GF option. Now just hang on a minute, here, I know that diners want to provide the best service and dining experience possible, but I didn't realise they'd branched out into offering girlfriends for you. Whose ideas was that? Maybe it was especially for Billy No Mates who comes in alone and sits at the stools. How would it work, then? If you asked for the GF option, were you given another menu to choose from? "I'll have the meatloaf, please, and can I dine with Lindy-Lou, 22, originally from Louisiana, her daddy is a truck driver, her mother sings in a jazz club and she wants to work with children and animals?" And would you have to buy their dinner for them, too? What about drinks? This was getting more difficult than we imagined it would. It turned out, though, according to the small print at the bottom of the menu, GF meant gluten free rather than girlfriend. Which, I have to say, was a relief. I mean, what would my wife had said when she saw the pictures?

"So, you went to Denny's then?"

"Yeah, it was really good in there."

"Looks like it. Who is this long legged, blonde haired, pouting Daisy Duke?"

"Oh, that's Lindy-Lou. She came with the meal."

It might have been a little bit awkward.

So, fortunately, it was just the two of us. I had a steak and Alex ordered a chicken skillet, and its the skillet that I need to focus on here. It was advertised as a 'sizzlin' skillet' and it certainly was. When it arrived it was bubbling away like a geyser about to erupt and we could have sent smoke signals with the steam rising from it. I have to say, it did look nice and when he took his first mouthful my suspicions of its tastiness were confirmed. "Ooooo," he summarised. It wasn't the most in depth food critique I had ever heard, but I certainly got the picture. In went the next mouthful closely followed by slow nodding of the head, eyes narrowed. It was a beautiful thing to see somebody enjoying their meal so much. But an even more beautiful thing happened when the waitress returned to check all was well.

Waitress: "Hey you guys, is everything ok with your meals?"

Me: "Yes, thank-you, very nice."

Alex: "Superb."

Waitress: "Awesome."

Alex: "This is the best meal I've had since we've been over here."

Waitress: "Seriously?"

Alex: "Seriously. This is just…"

…and he couldn't find the words to finish the sentence. There was nothing that would do his feelings justice, no superlative superb enough, no hyperbole hyperbolic enough. Instead, he just kissed the tips of his fingers and theatrically swept his arm upwards through the air the way a French chef would after creating another gastronomic masterpiece. It was a wonderful piece of theatre for which I had the privilege of a front row seat. But then, the pièce de resistance. "Let me get you a beer," offered the waitress, clearly overwhelmed by the pure ecstasy shown by her patron. And, sure enough, a moment later she was back with a bottle of Budweiser courtesy of Denny's Diner and a big cheery smile. Fantastic! That is what you call service.

Another thing I like about diners is some of the names they give to their plates of food. This is a particularly splendid thing with regard to the breakfasts. A glance down the menu sees such items as The All American Slam, Lumberjack Slam, Moons Over My Hammy, Wild West Omelette, The Super Bird, French Toast Slugger, T-Bone Steak And Eggs. No, wait, I must have accidentally gone over to the main meal section. Oh no I haven't, they are actually offering a 13 oz steak for breakfast with eggs done however you want. The picture also suggests that it comes with hash browns and toast. Who has steak for breakfast!? Steak is what you have for dinner, not breakfast.

Anyway, the names. The All American Slam – scrambled eggs with cheese, bacon, sausage, hash browns and toast. I guess that's the equivalent of a Full English Breakfast – fried eggs, sausages, bacon, tomatoes, mushrooms and toast. The Lumberjack Slam is what intrigued me, though. Presumably this is traditional lumberjack tucker. Every morning before heading out to the forest, all good and successful lumberjacks sit down at their breakfast table to tuck in to a plate of pancakes, ham, bacon, eggs, sausages, hash browns and toast. What, though, if the lumberjack in question also considers himself a good all American boy? Does that mean he has to have both the Lumberjack Slam and the All American Slam? My goodness me, how would he pack all that away? I suppose it would make felling trees a lot easier. After a few weeks of eating such a gargantuan repast every morning, all he would have to do is take a run at his chosen tree and watch it collapse under the weight. On top of that, imagine if he plied his lumberjacking skills in the wild west. He would also have to have a Wild West Omelette as well! Add to his daily morning feast another however many eggs went in to making the omelette, the filling of ham, peppers, onions and cheese as well as the statutory hash browns and toast, and I begin to feel sorry for the poor tress.

But even that pales into insignificance with what goes on at the place we ate at the previous evening. The All American Lumberjack Wild West Omelette Slam would have been nothing more than a mere starter for some of the people who frequent the Golden Corral. I don't know how highly this and other places like it rank on the American Sophisticated Fine Dining Gourmet Scale, but I suspect not too highly. The Golden Corral is a buffet. But to call it merely a buffet would be like calling Beethoven's Fifth Symphony a nice little tune. It'd be like calling the moon landing an interesting adventure. It'd be like calling Disney World something to keep the kids amused for an hour or two. I could go on but you get my point. The sheer size of it is astounding. You approach the buffet and take a selection of whatever you fancy (hey, come on, you know how a buffet works), and when you go to return to your table you realise there's another whole section you haven't visited yet. And then another. And then another. Think of some food, it'll be there. You purchase your plate for a menial amount of money and then you can just eat and eat and eat. This wouldn't be quite so bad if the patrons went and got and plate of salad and then a burger and chips and then a slice of carrot cake, for example, but there were people getting fried chicken, pot roast and ice cream on the same plate. Seriously, guys? You can visit the buffet as many times as you want, so why would you put together bizarre combinations that are clearly only designed to make you feel sick?

The thing is, though, it is just so compelling walking round and taking what you want and not having your mother slapping you on the back of the head telling you not to be so silly. It's like you've been let off the leash and you are free to do whatever you want. So actually, despite fighting against all you know is right, you do have a cheeseburger with an accompaniment of gumbo and M&Ms.

The biggest thumbs up for the Golden Corral is their steak. Oh man, it's good! There is a little serving station where the chef has a huge pile of meat, you can choose your own cut – as much or as little as you want – and he cooks it to your liking right there in front of you and it is just delicious. I've had steak that you've had to use a chainsaw to get through. I've had steak that is so tasteless you don't even realise you've eaten it. Here, though, it is fantastic. The knife just slides through it and your tastebuds party. It's fiesta time. You can almost hear them singing and cheering. If I'm ever on Death Row and I've been granted my last meal, I would ask to take it at the Golden Corral. This way there's a fair chance my guard will die of old age before I finished my last meal and I would be free!

Half an hour or so away from Kingman, we came to our favourite part of the entire journey road-wise. Following Historic Route 66, we came to a stretch called the Oatman Highway. Pretty much as soon as we hit the Highway the road got rougher and the cracks more prevalent. Either side of us there was nothing, just grass desert. If the road wasn't there it would have been easy to imagine a couple of cowboys slowly riding their horses towards the next town. Then, all of a sudden, the road became narrower with a lot more bends, some no more than hairpins. The road goes through the Black Mountains of Mohave County, and steadily rises, reaching an elevation of 3,500 feet above sea level at Sitgreaves Pass, the highest point of the entire route. Why it's called a 'pass' is anybody's guess because if any vehicle had come towards in the other direction there was seemingly no way it would be able to pass. One of us would have had to have two wheels on the road and two on the slope with the other as near to the precipice as they dare without tumbling over the edge. The hairpin bends had to be taken at no more than 20mph otherwise we would have been gonners. Fortunately, as it happened we were the only ones on the road for about 25 miles, the only other living things being the donkeys on the mountain side. At one point we did, in fact, see a car that had left the road and was now sitting smashed up half way down the mountain.

Back in the day, there used to be a little ice cream shop at the top of Sitgreaves Pass and drivers would often pay people to take them safely down to Oatman. Unsurprisingly, this part of the route was known for producing more than its fair share of wrecks, some of which were deadly, and became known as 'Bloody 66'. We survived, though, and agreed that the Oatman Highway was a brilliant piece of the route.

After the stomach-churning rollercoaster of the Sitgreaves Pass (ok, it wasn't *that* bad!), we came to Oatman itself. When we were there the population was two – me and Alex. Even the donkeys had left town. It was like we had arrived at a film set but it is a genuine old wild west town, complete with wagon wheels hanging outside the saloon and hitching rails to tie your horses up.

The first thing on the edge of town is the Oatman Mercantile, with a wooden sign outside giving a very brief history of the town. To borrow a little from said sign, "Oatman was founded about 1808 and by 1831 the area's mines had produced over 1.8 million ounces of gold. By the mid 1930s the boom was over and in 1942 the last remaining mines were closed as nonessential to the war effort. Burros first came to Oatman with early day prospectors. The animals were also used inside the mines for hauling rock and ore. Outside the mines, burros were used for hauling water and supplies. As the mines closed and people moved away the burros were released into the surrounding hills. The burros you meet today in Oatman, while descendants of domestic work animals, are themselves wild – they will bite and kick. Please keep a distance away from them. Wild burros are protected by federal law from capture, injury or harassment. Please help to protect these living symbols of the old west."

Well, it's a good job we didn't try to take one from the Sitgreaves Pass as a memento, wasn't it? Not only would it be a job to get through customs at LAX, but we would also have the feds after us. Of course, I would never deliberately injure any animal, but I did wonder what sort of harassment they have been subjected to. I wouldn't really fancy my chances if I tried to physically harass one – donkeys have notoriously hard kicks. Sexual harassment obviously doesn't even come into the equation, so that would leave phycological harassment. How would I psychologically harass a donkey?

Me :   "Oi, you."

Burro looks round...

Me :   "Yeah, you. Call yourself a donkey? Sorry, a *burro*...?"

Burro :

Me :   "Nothing to say, huh? No, I bet you haven't. You're not even a working animal, are you? What's the matter, don't you want to go down the mine? Scared of the dark, are you?"

Burro :

Me :   "Didn't think you'd have much to say. Your forefathers, they worked for a living, didn't they? You, though, you're a freeloader. Oh, yeah, that's right, a freeloader."

Burro :

Me :   "So what are you good for, then? Giving the little kids a
         ride at the seaside? Is that it? I bet you're slow as well,
         aren't you? Come on, let's have a race. You and me,
         here to the hotel, what do you reckon? I tell you what I
         reckon – I reckon you're scared. I'll even give you a ten
         yard start. Plus you've got twice the amount of legs that
         I have. Come on then, Mr Donkey, let's go…"

Burro : "Eeyore."

Burro just wanders off.

I have to point out at this stage that I didn't do that. There's no
way I would psychologically harass any animal. Certainly not
after what happened with that guinea pig, anyway. How can
something so small be so mentally tough? And who taught him to
play chess like that…?

Aside from the Mercantile, Oatman contained the Nugget Corral,
a saloon and pool hall, a theatre, a couple or trading posts, a hotel
and then we were out the other side. The hotel, incidentally, was
where Clark Gable and Carole Lombard honeymooned after
getting married in Kingman in 1939.

The town's name has an interesting story behind it. Jonny Moss,
the prospector who first discovered gold in the mountains, named
it after Olive Oatman, a young girl who, along with her sister
Mary Ann, was kidnapped by a group of Yavapais Native
Americans as their family headed to California from Illinois. The
Oatmans were approached by the group who asked for food and

tobacco. Their father, Royce Oatman, was loath to share their supplies and a fight broke out. Sadly, all the Oatmans were killed apart from three of the children, Olive, Mary Ann and their brother Lorenzo. He was left for dead and the two girls were taken to be slaves. After regaining consciousness, Lorenzo made it his goal to find and rescue his two siblings. In time, the Yavapais traded the two girls for some supplies and horses with the Mohave and they were taken in by the family of a tribal leader whose wife and daughter befriended them and they were given plots of land. They were even tattooed with tribal markings, indicating that they were on good terms. Unfortunately, Mary Ann died of starvation during a particularly heavy drought.

When Olive was 19, a messenger arrived at the Mohave camp from Fort Yuma in California, requesting to know if the rumours of a white girl living with the tribe where true and, if they were, that she be released. Eventually, after some negotiations, Olive was returned to the white man. She soon found out that her brother Lorenzo was alive and had been searching for her and her story made headline news across the west. A book about her was written and became the era's best seller, shifting more than 30,000 copies. Olive and Lorenzo embarked on publicity tours and Olive became a bit of a spectacle due to the tribal markings on her face. She went on to marry a cattleman called John Fairchild and they moved to Sherman, Texas.

Los Angeles

Not long after Oatman we crossed the Colorado River into California for the final leg of the journey. The road continued on in the same 'driving through wasteland' vein pretty much all the way to Barstow and our last bit of Historic 66 was the stretch leading us to San Bernardino. Cue the contrast. Having spent an awful lot of the western section of Route 66 in open fields, grassland and desert, passing small towns (by American standards) every so often, San Bernardino to Santa Monica was a different world. As we converged onto the freeway it seemed that everyone in the entire state was on the same road. Not just the city, the state! I cannot emphasize enough how mad San Bernardino to Los Angeles, the last 80 miles of the trip, really was. We seriously considered parking the car and walking the rest of the way as it surely would have been quicker.

San Bernardino, incidentally, was where the very first McDonald's Restaurant was opened. In 1937, brothers Richard and Maurice McDonald opened a food and drink stand they called The Airdrome in Monrovia, California. Three years later they moved their establishment to San Bernardino and renamed it McDonald's. Despite selling many different items, mostly barbecue, they noticed that most of their profits came from burgers. So, they temporarily closed their restaurant to remodel and rebrand it. The new menu, consisting of hamburgers, fries and milkshakes, became extremely popular and a legend was born.

Having taken what seemed as much time travelling from San Bernardino to Santa Monica as the rest of the route put together, we arrive at Santa Monica Pier. Obviously we can't drive onto the pier so we park across the road and walk the last 20 metres. The 'End Of Route 66' sign provided an exciting but also quite a sad sight. Sad only because that was it; no more traversing the country finding funny little places to stop, no more being just us, the car and the open road for miles on end. The sign is right outside Bubba Gump so it would have been churlish not to have treated ourselves to a shrimp dinner and a nice cool beer.

It seemed ironic that when we arrived in America for our trip one of the first things we did was visit the Navy Pier on Lake Michigan and now the end of the trip is signalled at another pier stretching into the Pacific Ocean. Just like it was in Chicago, Los Angeles is bathed in sunshine as, indeed, our entire journey had been. We had a wander along the pier, past the gift shops, restaurants of various types, ice cream stalls and the line of fishermen hoping to reel in as many sea bass, perch and mackerel as they could. The beautiful sandy beaches of Santa Monica Beach and Venice Beach were far too tempting for us not to walk along, although we decided against joining the joggers and speed skaters who seemed to be out in force. Just a leisurely stroll was enough for us, thank-you very much.

Our hotel for the final two nights of our trip was the Four Seasons in Beverly Hills. We had, after all, driven two and a half thousand miles, we thought we deserved a bit of indulgence to finish with. The marbled lobby set the tone of luxury, and our room was about three times the size of the others we had stayed in along the route. The views from the balcony gave us a panorama of Los Angeles, the famous Hollywood sign providing the backdrop. We took full advantage of the heated indoor pool with its poolside café, along with the spa and steam room. The cocktail lounge was an ideal way to spend the evening with the gentle music emanating from the piano player in the corner almost convincing us that we were actually extras in an old Hollywood production. Any minute now Humphrey Bogart and Audrey Hepburn would glide into the room and reminisce about old times before rekindling their hitherto long lost romance.

Oh, don't be ridiculous, of course we didn't stay there! We were, in fact, booked into the Dunes Inn on Sunset Boulevard which, actually, was very nice. I'm pleased we stayed on Sunset Boulevard because its just one of those places, isn't it? We walked along the famous Sunset Strip which became popular in the 1920s after a number of nightclubs and casinos opened up there and soon became a haunt of the movie stars of the 30s and 40s. By the 60s and 70s the Strip had fallen out of favour with the lights of the silver screen but the rock stars moved in and luminaries like Led Zeppelin and Frank Zappa played at Whisky A Go Go, with New York Dolls and The Stooges leading the new wave movement of the 70s. Plus, of course, the tv detective series '77 Sunset Strip' added to the lore (and in case you're wondering, that address doesn't exist – Sunset Strip address are four digits long). Nowadays the Strip is a lot more salubrious, with nice places to dine and fashion houses, although Whisky A Go Go is still there.

Los Angeles has an awful lot to offer. There's the neighbourhoods of Hollywood and Beverly Hills, the excitement given by Disneyland and Universal Studios, attractions like the Griffith Observatory and the Getty Centre. There is one thing, though, that Alex was absolutely desperate to go and see, and that was Angels' Flight. I'm going to be honest and say that I didn't know what Angels' Flight is. It turns out that it is a funicular railway and is, in fact, the shortest railway in the world. Costing only 50 cents a ride, it's length is just short of 300 feet. Apparently it had featured in the book he had been reading so, while we were here, we might as well pay a visit.

So through the traffic we struggled and then took ages to find somewhere to park. It was worth it, though, to see the excitement on his little face when the signpost pointed out that just across the road from the Grand Central Market was our destination. Now, just imagine the look on his little face when, after travelling 5,400 miles across the world, we found that it was closed for the day for renovation…

I really didn't want to laugh, honestly I didn't. And I tried my very best. That few seconds of silence went past. You know the ones. The ones where nobody dare say anything as the realisation of what has just happened sinks in. The ones where you just look at each other, eyes slightly widened, wondering who will break this awkward moment that seems to be frozen in time. The first voice was Alex's. "Noooooo!!!!" he cried before it became just that bid too much for me and I burst out laughing, slightly turning away in case he punched me in the face. Fortunately he didn't, although Los Angeles is the place to be if you need plastic surgery. Fortunately again, his next move was also to laugh and good spirits were restored. So back to the car we went and headed over to the Griffith Observatory instead. I'm so glad that he enjoyed looking round the Observatory. Imagine the atmosphere in the car if he had hated it...

Hollywood was the next stop on our whistle-stop tour of LA. Hollywood Boulevard runs parallel to Sunset Boulevard so we left the car at the motel and walked across. A saunter down the length of Hollywood Boulevard took us to the famous Chinese Theatre, Madame Tussauds, the Dolby Theatre, the Hollywood Museum and, of course, the Walk Of Fame. The idea for the Walk Of Fame came about in 1953 as, basically, a marketing ploy. The categories put forward for inductees were Motion Pictures, Television, Music Recording and Radio, with Live Theatre Performance not being added until 1984. To engender excitement for the project, eight stars were unveiled to the public as temporary measures in 1958 – those stars were for Olive Borden, Ronald Colman, Louise Fazenda, Preston Foster, Burt Lancaster, Edward Sedgwick, Ernest Torrence and Joanne Woodward. The project got the go-ahead and the first real star to be laid was in honour of the film director Stanley Kramer. There are now more than 2,500 stars, with 24 being added each year. The Walk Of Fame stretches along 15 blocks of Hollywood Boulevard and three blocks of the adjacent Vine Street.

The only thing left to do was climb the hills up to the famous Hollywood sign. We drove along Mulholland Drive as far as we could before the road came to an end. From then on it meant my taking a hiking trail around Hollywood Hills. I came to where the trail ended but wanted to get as near as I possibly could to those big white letters. I'm not entirely sure if I started to trespass on private property (if I did and the owners of that private property happen to be reading this, I'm sorry, I didn't realise) but it did look a touch like I might have gone a little further than technically allowed. The point at which I decided I couldn't really clamber any nearer was when the signs reading things like 'trespassers will be shot' started to appear. The only other people around were a man and woman who were looking as undecided as I was as to whether they were heading for a jail sentence or worse. We took pictures of each other to record the moment and headed back down to the road.

And that, dear reader, is pretty much that. Our adventure was over. 2,500 miles across the United States. The equivalent of driving, and this astounds me, from London, through the Channel Tunnel to France, through Belgium, Germany, Poland and Belarus, into Russia, through Moscow up to Kazan. I mean, who The following day we headed to LAX for our flight home. We did, of course, try the old "do you want us to take the Challenger back to the rent-a-car in Chicago" trick but sadly our services weren't required. One trans-Atlantic flight later and we were back at Heathrow.

4,000 miles from home and who do I bump into at the Painted Desert? My daughter!

Oatman. Unfortunately, no gold whilst we were there. Then again, there were no Dodge Challengers when the prospectors were there.

"A dead chicken for me, thanks. Sounds delicious."
The Snow Cap in Seligman and, below, Bone Daddy's. This
stretch of Route 66 is both bonkers and fantastic at the same time.

The Grand Canyon is the most impressive hole in the ground I've ever seen. The pictures do not do it justice - it is just stunning.

Hooray for Hollywood. The signs behind tell me that I will be shot if I try to get any closer. After some careful consideration I decided not to risk it.

Mission accomplished!

Elsewhere Along The Route

Of course, there were many places that we just didn't have time to stop at and explore, places that others conquering the route for themselves may well have checked out. To see everything we would have needed double the time we had. We would have loved to have had double the time we had, but that just wasn't practical or financially viable. So, just a word on some of the other towns and cities that are accessible from the Mother Road and have a bit of history to them…

Joliet, Illinois

Right at the start of the route, only 40 miles from Chicago, is the city of Joliet. Local landmarks include the Rialto Square Theatre, the Historical Museum and they also have a Route 66 Visitors' Centre. If you are to stop in Joliet, though, there are two things you must see, and they are the Rich And Creamy ice cream parlour and the local prison!

Joliet Prison is on Collins Street in the downtown district of Joliet. My suggestion is just to go and see the prison from the outside, don't actually rob a bank or set up an illegal moonshine stall in the hope of getting arrested just to see the prison's insides. It's the outside you would be interested in, especially if you are a film buff. The opening scene of the film The Blues Brothers, starring John Belushi as Jake Blues and Dan Aykroyd as Elwood

Blues, sees Jake being released from prison and being picked up by Elwood. That prison is none other than Joliet Prison. They then go on to embark on their adventures and, without giving away any spoilers, put a band together and have a right jolly old time. ("Without giving away spoilers"? What am I talking about? The film was released in 1980 for goodness sake!)

The Rich And Creamy ice cream parlour, on North Broadway Street alongside the Des Plaines River, is the place to go if you fancy an ice cream and, let's face it, who doesn't every now and then!? In case you're not sure which one it is, look for the bright pink ice cream cone and the models of the Blues Brothers on the roof. You can't miss it.

Cuba, Missouri

About an hour or so's drive from St Louis is Cuba. Colonised by the Spanish in the 15th century, it was then occupied by the United States in 1898 after the Spanish-American War. The Republic of Cuba was born after gaining independence in 1902 and came under military coup and dictatorship in 1952 under General Batista. He was ousted from power in 1959 and communist rule was established under Fidel Castro. Hang on a minute, this isn't right, is it? Sorry, I've got the wrong Cuba.

Let's try again...

About an hour or so's drive from St Louis is Cuba. This one was, in fact, named after the island of Cuba and contains one of the oldest motels on the entire route. Having opened in 1938, the Wagon Wheel Motel has continually served customers ever since. Originally consisting of three stone buildings providing accommodation and garages, there was also a restaurant and a filling station. The garages were soon converted into more rooms and, in 1963, the Motel was added to the US National Register Of Historic Places. The old filling station has now been converted into a gift shop.

Driving through Cuba you will also notice that there are a fair amount of murals dotted about the place. Amongst others, these include depictions of the actress Bette Davis to commemorate her visit to Cuba in 1948; members of the Osage Nation meeting French settlers in 1673; and one dedicated to the aviator Amelia Earhart who was forced into an unscheduled stop just outside Cuba in 1928. Four years later she became the first woman to fly solo across the Atlantic Ocean.

Another point of interest in Cuba in the Hayes Shoe Store, also the subject of a mural. The store displays a pair of shoes owned by Robert Wadlow, the tallest man since modern day records began. Wadlow, who was born in Alton, Illinois, stood at 8 feet 11 inches and his shoe size was 37AA by American measurements, 36 by British measurements.

<u>Tulsa, Oklahoma</u>

If, like me, you are interested in space exploration and science-fictiony type stuff, you may well wonder what it's like at the very centre of the universe. Would you just be destroyed as you are ripped apart by the various vacuums and galactic winds pulling you in all directions? Or would you be in a bubble of tranquillity as you exist unaging for ever more at the spot where time itself stands still? If you want to find the truth, then visit Tulsa. Yes, indeed, Tulsa, Oklahoma, contains the very centre of the universe. Before you slam this book shut refusing to read on due to my having gone completely tonto, please hear me out...

Situated just down the road from the Oklahoma Jazz Hall Of Fame, the centre of the universe is marked by a small brick circle. The spot is an acoustic anomaly. If you stand with both feet in the circle and make a sound, any sound, it is echoed back to you several times louder than you originally made it. For example, if you tapped the ground with your foot you would expect to hear the sound of your foot tapping the ground. Following me so far? Good. What you would actually hear, though, is the sound of your foot stamping on the ground. For some reason, you seem to be encased in your own personal amplifier. And here's the really weird bit ... anyone standing outside of the circle won't hear a thing! How mad is that?

Right on the outskirts of Tulsa is Catoosa, home of the famous blue whale. The blue whale was originally built in the 1972 by Hugh Davis as a surprise anniversary gift to his wife. I'm going to put my hand up here and confess that when considering what to get my wife as an anniversary present, a blue whale isn't normally towards the top of my list. It gets harder every year, I admit, but I wonder how long it would take me to run out of ideas so completely that the next obvious thing to surprise her with would be a blue whale. I have to say that I admire the man for even attempting to get away with it, but get away with it he did.

Prior to building the whale, Mr Davis had constructed two petting zoos, one filled with cats and the other filled with reptiles. He had also noticed that the pond near to their house often had children swimming in it so, as well as a gift for his wife, the blue whale also became a gift to the community as it provided an unusual slide and diving platform into the pond.

McLean, Texas

The land which would become the town on McLean was originally donated by and Englishman called Arthur Rowe in 1901. Named after Judge William McLean, the town grew rapidly and just three years later could boast three general stores, a bank, stables, wagon yards and it's own newspaper. Interestingly and sadly, Mr Rowe would later be one of the passengers who perished on the Titanic.

McLean is home to the Devil's Rope Museum. In case you didn't know, devil's rope is another name for barbed wire. You may well be asking yourself "how can there be an entire museum dedicated to barbed wire?", but there is, and it's here in McLean. I don't want to give too much away before you've had a chance to visit, but barbed wire as we know it today was invented by Joseph Glidden of Illinois. After many try-outs and experiments, he eventually came up with the design we all know and love. His design twisted a barbless wire around a barbed wire, thus doubling the strength of anything that had been used before. The thing is, everywhere you go on Earth, there's barbed wire, isn't there? Proving that Mr Glidden was actually a bit of a genius.

Gallup, New Mexico

Sometimes referred to as the 'Indian Capital Of The World', Gallup is in the heart of Native American lands, with the Navajo, Hopi and Zuni all having a big influence on the city's culture.

Gallup is also home to one of the famous hotels along the route, the El Rancho. Among the guest list you will find names like John Wayne, Ronald Reagan, Humphrey Bogart, Doris Day, etc. El Rancho was opened in 1937 as a base for local movie productions of the era. The rugged New Mexico terrain was popular among film makers of the 1940s and 50s, with many westerns being shot there including 'Billy The Kid' and 'Escape From For Bravo'.

Fort Wingate is also withing touching distance of Gallup. During the American Civil War, Military Commander General Carleton, in order to fend off the Navajo raids on New Mexico, built the fort, naming it after Captain Benjamin Wingate who had died during the Battle of Valverde. He rounded up the captured Navajo and relocated them to various concentration camps where many starved to death. Due to these atrocities, General Carleton was relieved of his duties and the surviving Navajo were released and allowed to return home. The fort was soon abandoned and now stands as a ruin.

Epilogue

So, there you have it. Bucket list, Route 66, tick. And what a brilliant experience it was. 'Get your kicks on Route 66' says the song and you know what? You do. You absolutely do. It seems to me that everything you need to know about America you will find along the route. Big cities? You got 'em. Try Chicago, St Louis, Oklahoma City and Los Angeles out for size. The Wild West? Just roll into Holbrook or old town Albuquerque. Prairie land? The drive from Oklahoma, through Texas into New Mexico should satisfy that need. Americana and just pure craziness? Move to Seligman or check out the Cadillac Ranch or the world's biggest fork. Yep, the Mother Road has it all. It's like you're actually on a tour of America through the ages. What I also liked about it was that the road was build around the terrain rather than through it. The interstates tend to just go through whatever is there, even if it means levelling the countryside or cutting through a mountain or whatever. Route 66, though, not only takes into consideration what was already there, but respects it. Hence we get twisty-turny stretches like the Oatman Highway. All this also adds to the experience.

Of course, when we got back home, many people asked us what the best bit was. That is impossible to say. There were so many things and places that we were really glad we saw, all of which have their own personality and charm. Plus, of course, what particularly appeals to one person might not mean a huge amount to another. That being the case, I will just list 10 things that, given our experience, anyone who does Route 66 really shouldn't miss out. I've omitted the Grand Canyon as it technically isn't on Route 66 but, obviously, this would absolutely be listed. I'm even going to list them alphabetically to avoid shouts of "favouritism"…

Bucket Of Blood Street, Holbrook
Cadillac Ranch, Amarillo
Delmar Loop, St Louis
Glenrio, Texas – New Mexico border
Land Run Monument, Oklahoma City
Navy Pier, Chicago
Painted Desert, Flagstaff
Route 66 Museum, Clinton
Santa Monica Beach, Santa Monica
Seligman, Arizona

So how would you prepare for a road trip? A certain amount of forward planning is involved, of course, such as the route, obviously, but too much planning can take the spontaneity out of it. Yes, we knew where we were stopping and one or two things to look out for, but there has to be a certain surprise to the proceedings. An obvious example for us was Seligman. Had I extensively researched everywhere before flying over, it would have taken half the fun out if it. As another example, I knew of the Cadillac Ranch but stopped myself looking up pictures so it was still a completely new experience.

An absolute must on any road trip is a decent soundtrack. There's nothing better than driving down a deserted road with beautiful scenery, the sun shining down on you and a cracking set of tunes to sing along to. Ok, you probably can think of a few things that are better than that, but you know exactly what I mean. You may have noticed that a couple of times throughout my ramblings I mentioned our Route 66 playlist. Before we left I put together a set of driving songs and those that were relevant to places we were to visit. Other tunes are available, of course, by here is our set list...

Living In America	James Brown
Hit The Road, Jack	Ray Charles
No Particular Place To Go	Chuck Berry
I Get Around	Beach Boys
2-4-6-8 Motorway	The Tom Robinson Band
Route 66	Chuck Berry
My Kind Of Town (Chicago)	Frank Sinatra
Walking To Missouri	Sammy Kaye
Kansas City	Little Richard
Oklahoma	The Cast Of Oklahoma
(Is This The Way To) Amarillo?	Tony Christie
The King Of Rock And Roll	Prefab Sprout
There Is No Arizona	Jamie O'Neal

California Dreaming	The Mammas And The Pappas
San Bernardino	Christie
California Sun	The Ramones
All I Wanna Do	Sheryl Crowe
L.A. Baby	The Jonas Brothers

Future road trips, then? I would love to. I have a few ideas but whether I'll ever get to do them is another thing altogether. What would I do next? Well, New England is appealing. Beautiful scenery, lots of history and some family ties, too (I'll tell all if I ever get to write it up). Following the trail of the Mississippi sounds interesting, tracing the river from it's beginnings in Minnesota right down to where it empties into the Gulf of Mexico in Louisiana. Then there's the Cowboy Land trip that I mentioned earlier. There are no doubt many wonderful sights, interesting places and completely mad things that are just waiting for me to discover them.

And I fully intend to...

Printed in Great Britain
by Amazon